GETTING BETTER

Getting Better

After the Death of a Loved One

Joan Liljedahl

This book was printed in the United States of America.

First Xlibris printing, January 2006

To order additional copies of this book, contact:
Xlibris Corporation
1-888-795-4274
www.Xlibris.com
Orders@Xlibris.com
31299

CONTENTS

Acknowledgments 9

Introduction   This One's For You 11

Chapter 1   "But I'm Really Not Ready . . . ." 15

Chapter 2   In The Beginning—Chaos 18

Chapter 3   You Don't Need Blood Everywhere To Feel Pain 29

Chapter 4   The Stresses In Specific Losses 40

Chapter 5   Grieving The Death Of The Unloving
             Grieving The Death Of The Reckless 50

Chapter 6   Coping With Children, Holidays, And
             The "Why?" Of It All 57

Chapter 7   When Others Let You Down
             When Others Lift You Up 68

Chapter 8   Good News—There's Help Around And Within 77

Chapter 9   Chaos To Renewal: When It Gets Better 82

Appendix I   Finding A Support Group 91

Appendix II   And Now For Your Story.................................... 93

DEDICATION

For the clients of Bereavement Services of the Hospice of Holy Cross Hospital, Silver Spring, Maryland, whose pain and courage inspired me to write this book, and to the grief counselors/group facilitators at the Hospice who encouraged me to proceed with publishing.

For our children, Katrina, Karl, and Greta who have loved and prevailed despite the staggering loss of their beloved brother, Eric.

For Eric, whose life has forever made this world a kinder and gentler place.

ACKNOWLEDGMENTS

I will be forever grateful to Sister Clarisse Belanger, former director of Bereavement Services at Holy Cross Hospital in Silver Spring, Maryland for her professional teaching and personal support and to my fellow counselors, especially, Teddy Handfield and her daughter Joanne, who validated the need for this book and encouraged my first effort.

Special thanks to my daughter Katrina who has urged this revision and helped so creatively and diligently with the final editing.

But the most loving and patient help came from my husband who coped with computer challenges and editing suggestions. Recalling in detail events to communicate them accurately was often surprisingly, overwhelmingly painful. I couldn't have coped without his hugs, ready offerings of tissues and compassion borne from our shared loss.

INTRODUCTION

THIS ONE'S FOR YOU

"He's passed on."

"She's gone."

"He's in a better place."

"We lost her."

"She expired."

I've never been comfortable with these common euphemisms we use when someone has died. Saying that someone "passed" sounds as if he's been suddenly relieved of a painful kidney stone. The other gentle phrase, "He expired," sounds to me like a library card or a driver's license we failed to renew or an outdated coupon we tried to redeem at the grocery.

To say, "We lost him," doesn't work either. I don't carelessly misplace people I love. I had no part in or control over his death when, in 1983, Eric, our nineteen year old son, the youngest of our four children, was killed in a fall. Still, I'm now resigned to using this way of telling someone about the saddest events in my life. So, I guess we "lost" Eric when he died. There it is, in a nutshell.

My mother died when I was in my twenties, and my father ten years later. I've lost an uncle and several aunts who were second parents and my younger cousin, Bill, who was as dear as any brother could have been, and a beloved brother-in law. Just as this book was being completed I have had to endure the sudden death of a beloved teen-aged granddaughter.

Since we've moved to a retirement community, I've grieved the loss of many new and valued friends. Still, each loss brings its own heartaches, and tears of sorrow!!

In 1983, we lived in Silver Spring, Maryland, where my husband was a research engineer for the U.S. Department of Agriculture at a nearby research center in Beltsville, Maryland. For over fifteen years I'd truly loved teaching high school English at a private boys' school in D.C. However, following Eric's death I returned to graduate school for a Masters degree in Pastoral Counseling, with a focus in the dynamics of loss and bereavement.

It was five years after his death before I felt ready to handle the emotional demands of grief counseling. Then, for the next twelve years I served as a volunteer bereavement counselor with the hospice program at Holy Cross Hospital when we lived in Silver Spring, Maryland. I had the rewarding experience of working primarily with groups of bereaved parents, children, and spouses.

But it's been my own inner wisdom that's helped me most in my grief odyssey. I learned to trust myself as I struggled to understand my reactions and emotions. Most of my own grieving was completed before I studied psychotherapy or worked with groups. I was able to ask myself the right questions, questions that helped me move through my grieving. It can be the same for you. Of course, I hope that the insight and encouragement shared in these pages, born of my own experiences of the many hundreds of courageous participants who have been in our groups, will help. I also hope you will trust the most valuable, unrecognized resource—yourself. If you must go through the anguish, you at least have the undeniable right to "tell it how it is" for you.

Thinking of you who must survive the first dreadful year after the death of a loved one, I've included things that might have helped me most twenty years ago when I struggled just to endure the year that seemed "out of time and space" following our Eric's death. Many fine bereavement books focus exclusively on the writer's story, detailing the daily struggle and events in his personal experience. Other books focus on a professional explanation of the grief process. I think we need both; I trust my personal story will make the "teaching" more relevant. I have also faithfully incorporated the voices of hundreds of people who, like you, have endured and yet survived such unbearable pain.

It's now been more than twenty years since Eric's death, even though I admit there are times when it seems like yesterday, so fresh and raw.

But I know that although Time can't change the loss or "heal" such deep wounds, I have found Time a kindly ally and welcome friend as I've coped with the unimaginable task of living a good life, good as it's been given.

However, over time our memories of events undergo subtle changes. In fact I know my children and husband would each have a very different story to tell, for their perceptions of that fragmented time are very personal and may be quite different. So don't be surprised if members of your family have different memories or "takes" on these overwhelming events.

During the first year, it is almost impossible to concentrate. I couldn't have focused on any demanding bereavement material during that fragile time. It was all I could do to check the day's date when I wrote acknowledgment letters for the many memorial contributions. So this is a book that you can read in a few short sittings. During the first year it's so easy to doubt yourself and your ability to survive. You may question decisions, mistrust instincts, and feel you must look exclusively to others for guidance. I 'm telling you that you already have your own wisdom, your own sense of what's best for you now. You will discover you are stronger than you ever believed; you just don't know it yet. And above all, you can trust yourself in this desperate quest to reclaim your life.

Finally, I'll address the many common experiences and reactions to loss that are not emphasized enough in other books because we find them distasteful or even taboo, such as grieving the death of an unloving person, or coping with people who fail you at this desperate time. Unfortunately, maintaining sanity while surviving the violent death of a loved one and the outrages of "Nine-eleven" and Hurricane Katrina are becoming more and more a tragic part of our national experience. Painful and outrageous as these situations may be, they are the reality we must somehow survive as we undertake the task of "getting better." And, of course, we're never ready, much less prepared.

An observant, sensitive new acquaintance who read an earlier version of this book enthusiastically suggested a new title, "Getting to the Other Side." As I mentioned this to my husband, I wondered if we ever get completely to the other side of our grief. His response was one of the greatest affirmations I could have as I re-worked this effort.

"Yes, you do get to the other side of sorrow, Joanie. Your book is to keep them from drowning on the way."

So, that's where we go from here. You head for shore, and I won't let you go under.

CHAPTER 1

"BUT I'M REALLY NOT READY . . . ."

A most beloved person in your life has just died, and you're starting one of life's most arduous and crucial tasks, the job of grieving. It's probably someone very close and dear, but it also may be a relationship that wasn't as close or special as you had hoped. The death may have been a sudden, catastrophic bolt from the blue or have followed a long, debilitating illness. No matter what the story, you probably never had any idea how terrible and lonely it is to miss someone so much, to know a pain so compelling and vicious. We're talking about a monumental struggle here, one that is often private and desperately lonely. It's as if a lovely excursion boat has just gone down with your loved one aboard, and you're floundering in murky, cold waters gasping for breath. And all you can think of in all the surounding chaos is the desperate, hopeless question, "What now? Where do I go from here?" Yet, impossible as it may seem at first, you can make good choices, and do more than just "survive." You are stronger than you know, wiser than you think. And so somehow you desperately head in the direction where the shore should be. And, the good news is that you can make it.

"BUT NO ONE TOLD ME IT WOULD BE LIKE THIS"

And, of course, you're never prepared when loss plunges you into a cauldron of confusion and emotional turmoil. There's no way you can possibly imagine or anticipate how completely devastating that will be. Someone remarked, "It's like having a rug you didn't even know was there suddenly pulled out from under you, sending you on a free fall into endless nothingness." I've never seen a simple check list in any of the popular magazines or cheerful brief advice columns on, "How to get over the loss of a loved one in ten easy steps." Of course, we all know better.

It can be something like the theater of the absurd. Suddenly you're on stage without a script, a director or a rehearsal, playing a part in a tragedy of numberless acts with no clue of how the plot line will actually unfold. And, if you're like many of us, you may still have certain expectations about how the "play" is supposed to proceed and how the characters are going to perform. Then, as the daily reality intrudes on these expectations, you discover unexpected conflicts and disillusionments that make your suffering even worse. You may blame yourself for the craziness and disappointment as if somehow you have failed to follow the script or adequately performed in this grief drama for which you never auditioned.

BUT WE WEREN'T CAREFULLY TAUGHT

Our anguish is intensified because we were not taught the facts of life about death. When we were young, we may have been excluded when there was a death in the family. We may have been confused and frightened, sure that something we did or some "bad" thought we harbored caused this catastrophe. No one took the time to sit down and explain just what was going on and address the scary thoughts that we didn't even have words for. School curricula recognize the need we all have for survival skills in sex and health education, home economics, child development, even financial management, but there are no classes explaining how to survive the major losses that will inevitably confront us in life. Most pregnant women attend classes *before* they deliver so they can understand and anticipate the rigors of childbirth, not *afterwards*. But, we have no preparation for the rigors and unyielding demands of grief before we are plunged into this labor that seems to have no end. We read the statistics and arguments for and against gun control, but no attention is given to "grief control" and the dangers we all face in harboring unresolved grief.

Since we're not taught how to cope with a staggering loss, our expectations about what should happen are OFTEN unrealistic. Furthermore, cultural traditions, and family expectations, well intended as they may be, can be misleading and stumbling blocks to our grieving. For example, movies and television dramas often suggest that this death crisis will bring our family together and make us closer than ever. This happens in many cases, but DON'T TAKE IT FOR GRANTED. At this time of exhaustion, and unwelcome decisions, past grievances may seem even worse and personality clashes intensified. "You always had to be the boss, to have it your way, and now you want to make all the plans for Dad's funeral," a younger brother may blow up as an older sibling assumes the burden of making funeral arrangements. "John always ignored unpleasant responsibilities, so it's really no wonder he's not here when we need his help." Family members may have limited ability to find the necessary patience or tolerance so desperately needed, which often puts marriages in jeopardy. People often land "lousy side up" at a time of crisis. We'll look at more of these misconceptions as we learn better ways to survive and overcome our debilitating and scary "first responses" to a heartbreaking loss. Then very slowly we'll get better.

CHAPTER 2

IN THE BEGINNING—CHAOS

"Things fall apart; the centre cannot hold;
Mere anarchy is loosed upon the world,
    From "The Second Coming" by William Butler Yeats

These lines, taken completely out of context from a poem, became a terrifying refrain when we learned of our son's death. It describes how we all feel when our world spins out of control, and we must combat the anarchy of emotional chaos when we hear the impossible words, "He died," or "She was killed." Suddenly, without any warning you lose your footing and plunge off the cliff of "reality" as you have always known it. Somewhere you're screaming, "It's not happening," "I can't believe I'm in the middle of this. This isn't supposed to happen; not to us, not to our family." Yet every story of loss is unique, an indelibly woven fabric in a family's history. Here's how it was for us.

ONE OF THOSE WONDERFUL JUNE DAYS

Our nineteen year old Eric felt he had the most wonderful job in the world the summer after his freshman year at the University of Maryland. He and three other college friends had formed a business that contracted to paint radio and television towers, an enterprise they had started the previous summer. They were all responsibly aware of the dangers inherent in this work, and besides, Eric's athletic coordination had always served him well in the climbing and outdoor activities he loved so much.

On a sunny June day I glanced briefly out our bathroom window before seven in the morning and saw Eric loading the last box of painting supplies into the back of our station wagon. I smiled at the energy and joy that vibrated in his every motion. How could I possibly know it would be the last time I would ever see my son alive?

He had good reasons for being especially happy that June 13. He had just received his freshman grades and was ecstatic he had received an A in his first engineering course, a grade that confirmed he really could handle the demands of the engineering program. Furthermore, he and his crew were about to complete a long project, located about a two hour drive from our home in Hagerstown, Maryland. Since it would be a short work day, they would be finished early enough to celebrate with dinner in a restaurant.

As coincidence would have it, two of the crew with whom Eric worked had the same given name. Whenever he phoned one of these friends, he'd announce, "Hi, this is Eric, Eric," I would never know which "Eric" he was addressing. Clearly the boys, savoring their special bonds of friendship, thought this was most clever.

Our younger daughter Greta was living at home then. Ten days before, we had all celebrated her BS/RN graduation from college. Since Eric had chosen to live at home and commute to school, the two had become especially close. At that time they had half seriously planned on doing missionary work, being the first "brother/sister" team, she in nursing and he in some engineering endeavor.

A SIMPLE PHONE CALL

Around noon we received the phone call that would forever change our lives. The call said that Eric Osborne, one of his friends on the job, had fallen and been killed. Greta took the hurried and rather incoherent call; there were no details. My husband Lou had just come by for a quick lunch. We couldn't comprehend what it was all about. Stunned and sickened at such preposterous news, we paced the kitchen, not knowing what do.

And then we started to worry about our own Eric. I could only imagine how shattering this would be for him. Since he had driven the three boys in our old station wagon that morning, I realized he would be driving the long heartbreaking trip back home. The thought of his driving the surviving stricken friend home under such stress unnerved me, but since the work site was on a mountain area, he couldn't be reached by phone, in those pre-cellphone days.

THE PLAN

So, we thoughtfully and meticulously formulated the plan for his return. It was decided that Greta would approach him first, with his Dad quietly available in the background. We thought he'd probably want to go directly to his own room. Since I was becoming emotionally distraught, it seemed best if I would sort of linger in the background and stay out of the way. We went over the sequence a few times before taking our assigned positions, stopping just short of a full dress rehearsal. Greta sat on the stoop outside our front door; my husband prowled the yard checking on weeds and ivy. And we waited and waited.

I did what I do best in times of great anxiety; I started to clean the living room. I thought about what I would say to Eric later. After much deliberation I felt calm enough to imagine saying, "Eric, honey, this is so scary for me, for us all. I can't think too clearly right now, but I know how responsible and careful you are and I trust you. If you choose to keep on in this job, that's O.K. with me. But now maybe you have some idea of just how terrible it would be for us if anything happened to you. Please just be extra careful. I couldn't bear to go through what's happening to your friend's parents right now." Having resolved this issue in my mind, I needed to call the pastor of the church near campus that Eric and his friends attended. Knowing how much Eric respected and trusted Rev. Knecht, I knew that a call or visit from his beloved pastor would be a great comfort. The church secretary assured me he would call as soon as he returned.

HOME AT LAST

So, we waited through the long afternoon, sitting, prowling, and cleaning. I dared not imagine what Eric Osborne's parents were going through. Finally we saw a state police car pull into our driveway, and, on cue, we put the carefully devised plan into action. Greta and Louie walked out to meet the shiny official car. I returned to my domestic chores in the back of our house overwhelmed with gratitude and relief as I assumed they persuaded Eric to leave our car at the worksite and had driven the grief stricken boys home. I even formulated the opening sentences of a thank you letter I'd send the police the next day. I was feeling so expansive I thought I might even send a copy to the newspaper.

But then, the plan seemed to have stalled. They were talking much longer out by the car than we had scheduled, clustered around the police car obscuring my view of Eric. I decided it was time to scrap the plan. After all, I had kept to my part and was curious about the details the police were probably explaining. So I approached the still group outside.

"Where's Eric?", I asked. "Didn't he come back with you guys?" Clearly, our plan was disrupted. Greta was leaning against her father, deathly still. My husband quietly and very carefully explained, "Honey, the police, they seem to have the idea it was our Eric who fell." These fine troopers had really botched it. We quickly persuaded them they were wrong, that one of the other "Erics" had fallen. As they came in the house to check back with the police in Hagerstown, I was simply distressed. By now it was late afternoon and Eric still had such a heartbreaking journey home in rush hour traffic. I scratched the idea of the letter of commendation. Their error made me a bit nervous, but I never for a second believed they were correct.

But correct they were. We never knew the cause of the communication mix-up, but when I heard the kind officer admonish his colleague on the phone, "Well, you'd better be sure on this identification because there's a family here that's going through hell." I knew.

Our son was dead.

A GLIMPSE OF HELL

And it was a descent into a hell. They say a drowning man sees his life flash before his eyes in the moment before death. At that moment, I saw all our future lives, lives without our Eric, flash before my eyes. Fragmented scenes of our daughter Katrina giving birth in two months to her second child, our younger daughter Greta and our other son Karl getting married and having children of their own, without the companionship of their brother flashed by. I saw my husband working in the yard and fussing over cars without the assistance of his ambitious helper. I saw family vacations at the beach with one of our family missing. I saw a parade of Christmases and birthdays and holidays forever tarnished and unblessed by Eric's presence. There was a flash vision of myself perhaps mourning the future event of my husband's death without the comfort of my son Eric, and even my own death without all my children to grieve for me the way it's supposed to be. For sure, it was a glimpse of Hell. With the slip of a foot, with a few words from a stranger, our family history was forever cleaved as surely as the historical notations of B.C. and A.D.

And, boy did we botch things up. Later that afternoon one of the other Erics returned our station wagon. I was in such a state when he handed me the car keys, I just nodded and closed the door, never thinking to ask him in, to have him tell us what happened, to offer him words of appreciation and comfort. Later Rev. Knecht returned our call. And, yes, we did have need of his services after all. We also had calls to make too, first to inform our oldest child, Katrina. We lived over an hour's drive from her house, so we called her husband and had him tell her. But, we should have been able to make the trip; we should have been the ones to break such unbearable news and comfort her. We just didn't or couldn't think straight and failed her. She had a toddler, almost two, and was expecting her second child in two months. But, her first "baby" had been her younger brother, Eric, who had been born when she was just six. Her marvelous maternal talents were first practiced by caring so happily for him. I myself never did learn to use a sewing machine, but despite that my older daughter acquired seamstress skills at an early age. So, naturally it was his older sister to whom Eric took any sewing requests. It was she naturally who helped him fashion his Halloween costumes.

We also had to call our older son, Karl and tell him that the boy who used to call him "big bro" had died. There were no family members with Karl to help cushion the cruel news. He assured us he had a friend he could talk to and he'd return home from New Jersey the next day.

On the coming Saturday, only four days away, we had made plans to hostess an "end of the year" celebration cook-out for the faculty of the private school where I taught. For a few minutes I actually thought that we could carry on and get things ready by then. There seemed no reason to reschedule. Then, the thought did occur to me that perhaps we might be too busy with some kind of funeral stuff in the next few days and it would be rushing things to still prepare for this party. Little did I know or imagine what lay ahead. I didn't even realize how crazy my thinking was.

MANAGING SO WELL . . . . AT FIRST

During the next weeks, I kept thinking about the book "Winnie the Pooh," the part where Pooh-bear is carried off, borne aloft by the many balloons he has clutched in his hand. I feared I would be carried off like that, doomed to drift forever, ungrounded and lost. There was one way I could force myself to stay grounded, and that was to hear myself say the terrible words, "Our son was killed." The pain of saying those words sort of punctured the balloons that threatened to carry me away forever. People would wince and shudder at my pronouncement, yet I took a rather perverse pleasure in their discomfort. After all, if I was doomed to this reality forever, they could darn well submit to a temporary flicker of pain. Of course, this thinking doesn't make sense, perhaps, but nothing has to make sense at first; and after all, there is no sense in the horror of it all anyhow.

Yet our family managed heroically. It was amazing how competently we managed during those first unreal weeks. My husband handled all business necessities, our daughter Greta, "the other Erics," and Eric's pastor worked on the memorial service. We never failed to encourage and comfort those who came to offer their condolences. We wrote hundreds of letters thanking people for their contributions to Eric's memorial fund. Many contributions were from his friends at school, at church, contacts from his work the previous year at a Young Life camp, or teammates on the three volley ball teams he played on. Greta did well on her nursing boards on July 13, exactly a month after his death. But she was smart enough to know she was in no shape to start her nursing job that required such diligence and concentration and arranged to start at a later time. During those summer months, I'm sure the world was as impressed as I was by how well we were handling it all.

HITTING THE WALL: CRISIS AT THREE MONTHS

Yes, we were doing so well, and then, about three months later, the pain seemed so much worse. It was as if we had hit some powerful invisible wall, as if we had been sheltered by the calm eye of a hurricane and were suddenly thrust into unexpected, unrelenting Category Five forces, surrounded by the wreckage of our lives without Eric. We were experiencing the "reality" wall that most bereaved people predictably encounter after three or four months.

Actually, we'd been mercifully cushioned by shock, and denial for the early weeks. Now, as that wore off, we had to confront the finality, the "foreverness", the long term consequences of his death. The early month seem to encompasses a season in a year, and the rest of the world, reassured by how well we're doing, now considers our loss "past history" and sees no need for further involvement.

Maybe you also managed magnificently in the weeks following your loss. You might have had some of the same reactions and feelings that I and so many others I've talked to have known. We can manage so well that the world acknowledges our capabilities and courage and assumes—incorrectly, of course—that we're getting over it. Since we're so strong, they don't have to worry about us. Now they can exhale.

THE TERROR SETS IN

Actually, we were not really doing as well as appearances might have suggested, as others might have wanted to believe. Underneath the surface of such fine coping, is a cold, implacable terror. At first there is the terror that you will never physically live through the pain. Later there's the greater terror that you will survive and be doomed to live forever with unbearable sorrow. Since you've no idea what to expect or where you go from here, it's pretty natural to think you're going crazy.

To the contrary, this is also a season of necessary progress; the movement from "protective novocaine" to reality check is crucial movement toward recovery. Don't be panicky. One young man joined one of our groups three months after the sudden death of his Mom. Clearly overwhelmed by his grief, he explained, "I've always been absolutely meticulous in balancing my check book every month. If I was a penny off, I'd go back and check it over and over until I got that bank book to balance. Since my Mom died I haven't even tried to balance my check book, I can't do it. In fact I have no idea what my balance is," he despaired. It had been several weeks and his inability to concentrate was a normal response to the three month crisis.

THE CRAZIES

In the bereavement groups which I had led for the past 12 years, almost everyone confessed that in the early weeks they harbored secret fears they were going crazy, becoming unbalanced. It wasn't funny; it was simply frightening. Here are the most common complaints:

I can't sleep.

I sleep too much.

I can't concentrate on anything.

I wander from room to room and have several things going at once, but I can't complete anything and forget what I'm supposed to be doing. Nothing gets finished.

I hear my dear one's voice from the grave. I'm sure I see her at times, the presence is so real.

I cry at the dumbest things and at unexpected times.

I can't cry; maybe I should cry more.

I'm so exhausted. There's no energy anywhere.

To be honest, I wouldn't mind it if I got sick and died, anything to get away from it all.

I seem to have forgotten how to write checks.

I fly off the handle at everyone, I'm so irritable I can't see how people stand me.

I'm in a constant state of panic.

I couldn't breathe and had such chest pain they took me to the emergency room; but it wasn't a heart attack, it was nerves.

This isn't like me. I don't even know myself. It's as if an alien force has taken over my body.

Such a list could go on and on and on.

But what these people experienced were the normal initial responses to loss. By "normal" I simply mean if you have these feelings you're not crazy and you don't have to be scared by what's happening. You are a **normal** person experiencing all of the confusing, frightening reactions to the shock of loss—reactions that we all have. In painful medical situations, as the days following a knee replacement or during the agony of childbirth, nurses quite cheerfully assure us that our "discomfort is quite normal and expected." That may be true, but four letter words like "pain" and "hurt" still describe our reality. In grief as well, "normal" doesn't mean it's painless; it hurts, and we need to talk about this pain over and over.

We each have our own story of the "normal crazies" we endured at this time. A friend of mine recalls her anger at her family because she couldn't find her pocketbook a few weeks after her husband's sudden death. "I was fussing at everyone, looking for that purse, having them look with me, and then I finally found it—in the freezer." She can laugh now when she recounts the story, but it wasn't funny then, not at all.

LOSING IT AT THE SUPERMARKET

I had my own episode of craziness. About three weeks after Eric's death I had to go to the grocery store. I always shop from a list, quickly and efficiently. I should have known I was in trouble as I made the list. As Greta helped me it seemed as if most of the things on the list were the usual snacks and food items I'd always get for a hungry teen-age boy and his friends. Greta wailed, "Oh, we'll never be able to make brownies again", as she thought of her younger brother's favorite dessert. I didn't have a long list, for our refrigerator was still quite full of the many meals that people had brought. So, I headed to the super market prepared for a quick trip.

As soon as I entered the store, things seemed wrong. The lights were too bright and hurt my eyes. And, although it was early afternoon and uncrowded, there was so much confusion, and noisy, abrasive sounds. I followed my list through the first section and then came to the aisle that had canned tuna fish. Tuna fish was Eric's favorite, favorite food. You would have thought the cans were going to attack me. I panicked. I simply could not go down that aisle. Now, that's all I remember about that quick shopping trip. I did go home and immediately went to the bedroom and cried and cried, finally dozing off.

I was wakened by Greta's knocking on the door and rather tentative questioning. "Mom, Mom, is it all right for us to unpack the groceries in the hall?" Apparently I had just brought them in and left them there. I called out, "Sure, go ahead, honey." As I entered the front hall I saw Greta and my poor husband struggling to carry some twenty bags of groceries into the kitchen. "Honey," my husband asked diplomatically, "I assume you have some plan for these?" "I don't remember getting any of this stuff," I gasped. I gasped even more when I examined the checkout tape of groceries totaling hundreds of dollars. There were items there I never had bought before, like various motor oils and bags of charcoal, when we had no cook out plans. There was a huge turkey (and I don't feel confident cooking turkeys even on Thanksgiving), a ten pound bag of rice, even baby food when we hadn't had a baby in the house for nineteen years. I stood there stricken and helpless. My husband suggested I just pick out the items I wanted, and then they bagged up the rest and returned them. The store manager was very understanding.

But I never did figure out what happened. I was bewildered but didn't sense how really crazily I had acted. It seemed as if I had purchased every item in the store except tuna fish. Perhaps I just bought one of everything to be sure I could provide for my family and keep them safe. Perhaps I bought everything possible so I'd never have to grocery shop again. I'll never know. Years later, however, as I woke up in the hospital recovery room following a general anesthesia, I had the same sensation. Lights too bright, voices too loud, too much confusion. Perhaps the act of grocery shopping was a bit like coming out of the "anesthesia" immediately following his death and slowly forging a panicky adjustment to the real world.

It was a bizarre, psychotic episode. It's funny now, and I know it was a normal part of early bereavement, but back then, it wasn't funny.

HE CAN'T REALLY BE DEAD

Perhaps one reason it can be so crazy is the mechanism of denial that takes over. And, in situations of sudden death, it takes especially long for it to become real. The fall after his accident, I somehow still expected Eric to return in time to register for his classes. It seemed inconsiderate for the University to hold classes without him! Eric and I were the wild and crazy football fans in our family. I turned the television off after the first ten minutes of the first Washington Redskin game that fall and never did remember who they played or if they won or not. I was offended that the teams even played. Surely the NFL would postpone the season if they couldn't have the participation of their wildest fan!

A girl in one of our bereavement groups whose mother had died a few weeks previously, told us of continuing to attempt her usual long distance calls to her Mom, until the phone was disconnected. She slowly and quietly admitted, "I had to realize that maybe she was really dead after all."

The tears come and come, even at unexpected times. At first there's the fear that if you start crying, you'll never be able to stop. About two weeks after his death, the closing hymn at our Sunday church service was *God Be With You Till We Meet Again*. I sobbed and sobbed. As my feeble efforts to compose myself failed, I finally gave up. "Oh, the hell with it," was my impious thought as I kept on sobbing. During those early months I harbored the thought that I would cry so uncontrollably, that, like the Sorcerer's Apprentice, my tears would unleash a tidal wave that would wash everyone out of church. I pictured our congregation washed down the aisle in the resulting torrent. The headlines would read, "Woman's tears cause flooding at local church. Red Cross alerted."

In a few weeks, as I became more comfortable with the pattern of my own crying, I was relieved to find that I could break down briefly in public and then get back on track. I soon learned that tears did not destroy. Tears helped heal. I advise you to keep lots of tissue around. Keep tissues in every pocket, and always have a box next to the driver's seat in your car. In other words, never leave home without it.

And so, shakily, we all somehow stagger through the bizarre, early unfocused weeks. I missed our Eric beyond the telling of it. The overpowering feelings of pain, despair or anger took up all the space. It seemed as if it would always be like this. I couldn't even imagine, much less believe, it could ever change. But in the first phase of raw grief, you are beginning a process that will lead to healing, to getting better. All you have to do, at first, is just hang on. Just surviving is a victory.

CHAPTER 3

YOU DON'T NEED BLOOD EVERYWHERE TO FEEL PAIN

With the slip of a power saw a young man we'll call Mugs severely cuts his hand, down to bare bone. The sudden spurt of blood and unbelievable pain tell him something is really wrong, and he immediately seeks help for this physical medical emergency. Physicians examine the injury to determine what's wrong so they can do whatever is possible to help it heal. When a loved one dies, there are wounds to the very core of our being that are just as deep, yet there are no visible signs of "blood and gore." In the previous chapter I've described the shock and denial so characteristic of the first phase of grieving. It can seem a time of numbness as if you're perched on a ledge observing, in a rather detached manner, your performance below. Detached, that is, until you finally sense that the unbearable sorrow is here to stay and you must somehow make it bearable or perish. Instead of bandages, stitches, and splints, you must rely entirely on words that speak of the pain beyond language. And these words are words about feelings.

AND NOW—ON TO PHASE TWO

Thus you stumble reluctantly into the second phase of grieving, acknowledging and communicating the feelings of loss. Every book on bereavement, and the experiences of countless sufferers like you and me, indicate there are three inescapable, major progressions in our grieving. This second phase is perhaps the most painful as you undertake the main task of grief. It can take at least a year, probably much longer; it always seems unfairly slow. It's like your tongue can't help exploring the hole where your extracted tooth was, or the "phantom" pain that may accompany an amputation, while you must learn a new way of life that accommodates to such wrenching change. However, you will get through it in the time frame necessary for your own recovery. The challenge for now is to find the words that work for you. We're talking here of raw, intense emotions, for we are never prepared for such depths of pain and anger.

When we're children, our real feelings were often denied or just ignored. Listen to some familiar dialogues from back when . . .

CHILD: "I'm so mad I didn't get the prize. It's not fair."
ADULT: "Now, Tommy, you can't expect to have things fair all the time. It doesn't do any good to get all mad about it."

CHILD: "I'm crying because I'm sad that Rover had to die. I miss him."
ADULT: "Your doggie died a long time ago, honey. Let's think about some good things that make us happy."

CHILD: "I don't want to get a shot at the doctor's. I'm scared."
ADULT: "Big boys like you don't need to cry about that. You're old enough to be brave like Daddy."

Is it any wonder when we face, perhaps for the first time in our lives, the most intense, frightening emotions we have ever known, that we're reluctant to claim them for ourselves? Is it so surprising we so often let others determine their worth or appropriateness? So, where do we go from here? We talk about our feelings for ourselves.

Here's a partial list of feelings people most often confront at a time of loss:

> anger, guilt, depression, sadness, despair, fear, anxiety,
> fatigue, betrayal, irritable, jealousy, envy, hate, relief.

You probably have your own to add. These feelings are human; they make us real. Having "bad" or "negative" feelings doesn't make us "bad" people no matter what the voices of childhood have told us. What we do with them, how we choose to act on them is a choice we do have, a choice that can work for our own good or hamper our recovery. Very often, just "naming" the feeling, saying it out loud gives us some power over it.

Here are a few of the common emotional reactions that we must often handle as we slowly get better.

FEAR

Fear comes in all sizes, from a pervasive feeling of uneasiness to full blown panic. A man whose wife suddenly died of an aneurysm while they were watching television reported that he was always scared. "It's like . . . in this house where Beth died, something or someone's ghost that's just waiting to jump out at me. Sort of like Halloween." And there can be a constant worry for the health and safety of other loved ones. Your concerns when a family member is late coming home is no longer a casual awareness, but assumes life and death proportions. And the worst fear is that you'll always be in this "never never" land of unnamed terror. But this won't last forever, even if it seems that way.

ANGER, THE "A" WORD.

The anger and rage can splatter all over. There's anger at the loved one who seems to have abandoned us to this uncomfortable new world. There's anger at God who let this happen, anger at the rotten unfairness of it all, anger at others who have the effrontery to live happy lives in their safe worlds. There's anger at the medical community, anger at friends and relatives who hurt our feelings, even anger at ourselves for feeling such rage when we've been so carefully taught that anger is unbecoming. Those who are divorced or widowed report being furious when friends complain incessantly about the shortcomings and petty irritations of their spouses. In the fall after Eric's death, I saw a group of three high school boys standing indolently on the corner. It looked to me as if they were skipping school and probably smoking "weed". How dare they be so sullen, so derelict, so irresponsible when good, dependable kids like our Eric weren't here? It took monumental restraint not to jump out of the car and shake them till their teeth rattled.

There's no law that says you have to be angry, but if that's the way you feel you are entitled to talk about it. It helps to recognize that anger is often the result of fear, when we feel terribly threatened or powerless at the terrifying "unfairness of it all." Of course, there was no real reason for me to be angry at the boys on the corner. They were just hanging out and kidding as boys do. I was simply heartbroken knowing our son couldn't ever be part of that carefree life; that he couldn't be alive. Anger at insensitive health providers may be justified, but the deeper anger is perhaps that they were powerless to save a life of someone so precious to us. And sometimes we don't even know where the anger belongs. It just sort of lurks there in the pit of our stomach.

GUILT-THE BIG "G"

Another inevitable, troublesome reaction is guilt. Big guilts, little guilts; they all matter. For example, my mother had been a model before her marriage. She really had a tall, willowy model's build and managed to always dress so stylishly, and look like a million despite the meager clothes budget she'd allow herself. After she died, I really felt terrible that I hadn't complimented her more. I just always took it for granted that my Mom would be the most striking one at any gathering, but why, for heaven's sake, hadn't I told her that?

I remember our last visit with my beloved Aunt Ruth in Rochester, Minnesota, a few weeks before her death. We had said all our good byes and hugged, but as my husband and I left her room ready for the long drive back to Maryland, I glanced back and just glimpsed such a forlorn expression on her face, like a child we'd just left at camp, and I wished I'd gone back for one more hug and, "I love you." Oh, how we wish we had these second chances to be perfect.

A lady in one of our spousal loss bereavement groups had lovingly and faithfully attended her husband through a long, debilitating illness. During the final days of his illness, he murmured something about loving the favorite sourdough bread she'd always made. Of course she couldn't leave his side to go shopping and then go home to make the bread; furthermore, at this stage of his illness he couldn't take any nourishment by mouth anyhow. But, you guessed it, months after his death she was still confessing, "I feel so guilty that I never did make that sourdough bread he wanted."

Here are some other very, very common guilt thoughts many have. It's almost as if you can't win. No matter what you did or didn't do, it feels as if you messed up.

"We should have taken our long awaited trip before he started chemotherapy and got so sick."

"We should have just stayed here and started treatment immediately. Maybe that would have saved him."

"I shouldn't have let him go to the store for me when the weather was bad."

"If I'd just been a better son, my dad would have been happier."

"I should have insisted she get a complete check up earlier even though she refused."

"I feel so bad because I DON'T feel any guilt about my Dad's death. Maybe something's wrong with me." (Just try to figure that one out. It's not an uncommon confession.)

The list of "should haves," and "ought to's" goes on and on, as if we alone had the power to change the course of events, when the awful reality is that there were probably many other events leading to or causing these deaths that never were in our control.

We too had to wrestle with the guilt that we'd allowed our son to do such dangerous work, a decision many friends had questioned or wondered about in the previous year. "Dear God, how could we have allowed our precious son to be in such jeopardy? Why didn't we realize the risk was just too great?" But, our salvation lay in the fact that we were able to ask ourselves the right question. "If we are guilty in his death, whose forgiveness do we need?" The healing answer came immediately. The person whose forgiveness we'd require was Eric's, and we had that forgiveness years ago, before his first day on the job. From the time he was able to walk, he loved to climb, demanded tree houses, and joyously sought out mountains and rock faces to test his abilities. We knew he respected our concerns for his safety and was especially careful and responsible. But most importantly, we respected his love for what he did. How unfair it would have been to him for us to feel guilty about his wonderful choice. By asking ourselves the right question, guilt was no longer part of the picture.

THE GUILT TRIP WHEN RELATIONSHIPS WEREN'T SO GREAT

But what about the long term guilt when a relationship has not been so happy or so good? I think most families are to some extent "dysfunctional," but it's harder for some to cope than others. My father was an alcoholic, and my mother struggled wonderfully and valiantly and alone to make things work. However, as the oldest of three girls, she always seemed to expect me to be the savior. The message was so often, "You're just like your father, all you do is read. If you were a better sister, things would be so much easier for your sisters. If you wouldn't stay in your room all the time, we could be a family." It wasn't until several years after her death that I realized how unrealistic and unfair her expectations were. And then the sense of oppressive guilt and responsibility faded to be replaced by simple feelings of remorse. For me, remorse means that it's too bad, it's sad that it was that way, that things couldn't be different. Remorse assigns no blame.

Remember, it takes two to form a relationship. One person does not always have the power to determine how things work out. Guilt seems to say we had all the choices to make things different, to change lives, to make others happy and safe. Guilt says we should be omnipotent and have known the absolutely right thing to do or say. Actually, it's important to look back at the "should" and "what ifs" and realize that back then, at that time, we probably did the best we could. It's irrelevant whether decisions and actions were right or wrong, whether they made any difference. What is relevant is that we mere mortals made the best choices we could, being who we were and knowing what we did then. Believing this, we can gradually absolve ourselves of our requirement to have been perfect and all knowing.

Finally grief is not like a sudden storm or getting over chicken-pox. We can't just stay inside or in bed for awhile and expect the pain to pass away in a few days. In fact, our task, unwelcome as it may be, is to forge a new "reality," our brave new world without the loved one's presence.

OTHER FEELINGS THAT CAN MAKE US FEEL BAD

Grieving is amazingly exhausting, physically, spiritually, and emotionally. So we're not in top shape to cope with more feelings that intrude and attack us in this vulnerable state. No wonder so many struggle with an uncharacteristic lack of confidence and low self-esteem. It might not make sense, but so often an overall sense of failure, that we should have been able to do something, to keep a loved one safe takes over. After all a necessary crucial part of you has been amputated. Now, you're not even whole. To make it even worse, we may experience negative feelings that encourage us to feel even worse about ourselves.

But remember, just having a bad feeling doesn't make you a bad person. Many experience major depression for the first time following a major loss. Loss of interest in usual activities, lack of energy, inability to concentrate, feelings of hopelessness and despair are all part of the picture. Usually, as you keep active and busy day by day, allowing time to talk to others and share the sadness, the depression will gradually lift.

Feeling jealous doesn't mean you're a "green-eyed monster" either. It's natural and all right to feel jealous when your friends have caring parents and yours are gone, to envy couples planning retirement activities when your spouse's death denies you the same joy. Once after my father's death, a good friend innocently recounted stories of fishing trips she used to have with her father. A flash of jealously whipped through me. In the first place I could hardly imagine what it would be like to have a Dad like that. And I didn't want to hear or be happy for her memories.

It's understandable to know relief, or happiness, at a time that's supposed to be devoted to sorrow. Relief that a loved one no longer suffers is acceptable, of course. But we're also allowed our own relief that we no longer have to care for him, worry about him, or keep witnessing his decline. There's understandable relief when the critical, demanding voice of a controlling parent or spouse is finally stilled. It's only human to have an inner voice that yearns to shout, "Free at last. Thank God almighty, I'm free at last." When death brings us freedom to move on, to make choices long denied, we can rejoice without getting tangled up in the "BIG G" trip.

The good news is that feelings aren't carved in stone, that feelings change. As we progress in our grief, we may find they don't stay as heavy, as dark and overpowering as they did at first. You may be barely hanging on to the shreds of an old life raft, but you sense you're going in the right direction and feel confident in the shore just out of sight. When rage at my father eventually mellowed to sadness, and guilt at my mother's death softened to remorse, I knew I was truly a wiser person: I could finally exhale.

NEWS FLASH FOR MEN

Here's a news bulletin. Men are also allowed the emotions of grief. A man's pain isn't less important or severe because he may have a greater capacity to mask it. It's there, demanding to be acknowledged rather than buried. To cope with loss, a man may desperately work to "do" something, to "fix" it for those he loves. But this may be the first time in his life when he can't be in control or negotiate a workable plan for "solving a problem." So, it's imperative that he find out what "works for him": he may need to be alone and deal with his grief in private, work out his anger with physical activities, or find someone to talk to about the emotions that can be unbearable for us all.

Any physical activity or exercise is especially helpful for men. The summer Eric died, my husband and I would go to the tennis courts presumably to play tennis. Well, all we really did was to attack and smash balls across the court. I don't think we ever had a rally. We didn't keep score . . . we just loaded our poor rackets with all the pain and grief in a futile effort to literally smash the balls to death. But, the physical release of energy was good: we were both scoreless winners.

Even if "talking about feelings" isn't your bag, I urge men to check out bereavement support groups. The beauty of these is that you will be with total strangers who have no connection with your work, or your fishing or hunting buddies or your golf bunch. This anonymity and confidentiality makes it much easier to talk and be "real."

During the first summer Olympics following Eric's death, I was wistfully watching the beach volley ball competition. Remembering how skilled he had been, participating on several community and school teams during the year, I sighed, "Gee, Eric would have loved this."

"I don't see how you can stand to watch that," observed my husband as he broke into tears and left the room. Later he calmly yet sadly explained. "I just can't watch volley ball games. I've also given up watching ski competitions. Eric also loved skiing. I can't stand his missing it." John Walsh didn't deny the American public the opportunity to see and learn of his grief during the years following his young son Adam's disappearance and brutal murder. His founding of the national foundation for lost and exploited children was something productive he could offer from such pain.

Believe me, "masculinity" is the strength men display in gentleness, the power they have in risking vulnerability. Real men can shed tears.

HELPING YOUR SPOUSE TO GRIEVE

The bottom line here is to respect the reality that we grieve differently and on our own timetable. So please let your spouse do it his way and allow space for this great task. It may stretch your patience if he wants to talk about the loss nearly 24/7, but it won't last forever. If he needs solitude and time alone, help provide opportunities for that healing.

Yet, despite their own anguish, there are so many men whose remarkable sensitivity and creativity help cushion our grief in loving ways. During the weeks following Eric's death, my husband would usually leave work and drop by for lunch. He'd usually bring in the day's mail and we'd look at the cards, perhaps cry, and decide which ones needed some response. He had even written an introductory sentence or two with which we could preface most correspondence. After he returned to work, I'd go ahead and write the letters, grateful to have something to occupy my time. Of course I realized much later that his lunch visits were not accidental, but rather timed to coincide with our mail delivery so I wouldn't have to open them alone. What a difference his presence made.

A few years later, in the weeks following the ever painful date of Eric's birthday I noticed Katrina had a new chair in the living room. She loved interior decorating and arranging furniture and stuff like that, but with a growing family there just wasn't money to indulge in that luxury.

She explained. "Bob knows how awful the month of March is for me with Eric's birthday. Well, the year after Eric's death, Bob started a secret decorating account for me so every March I could plan and do some small thing for our home. It was so sweet and I love that he cared. You know he really loved Eric too." It wasn't a fantastic amount; it was sacrificially budgeted, but it was one of the most loving, sensitive gestures anyone could offer. And it was a "guy thing."

Our daughter Greta had been seriously dating a young doctor who would be her future husband. They stopped by our house on an anniversary of Eric's birthday. After they had visited for a short time, Greta apparently went to another part of the house and Kevin joined me where I sat in the kitchen numb with misery on this worst day of the year. He simply knelt beside my chair and said, "Greta's told me so much about Eric and how close they were." I could only choke out the words,"It's a bad day, his birthday." Kevin gently patted my shoulder and said, "It must be. How I wish I'd had a chance to know him." After a few quiet moments, he got up and went to seek Greta.

That was just the balm I needed, words of understanding and compassion from a man who had never known Eric, but knew the right words of comfort.

THE PUBLIC FACE OF GRIEF

We all recall occasions when a well known public figure has died and, thanks to the ever attentive media scrutiny, we can observe, up close and personal, the family members as they participate bravely, with enviable composure, in funeral activities. We may remember Princess Di's sons on their restrained, disciplined, pilgrimage behind her casket on the way to the service. At the time of Pope John Paul II's death, all the priests and bishops I saw interviewed calmly and gently focused on how great the Pope's contributions had been and how difficult it would be to replace him. But I saw one young priest who revealed his personal grief. "He's been our Pope all of my life. I just think of him as my own father," he said brokenly as he struggled in vain to hold back tears. Then his composure returned.

However, public mourning and private grieving are not the same. You were witnessing the rituals and behavior of their "mourning", their ability to put personal grief aside so they could shepherd us the public through such stressful times.

You too may have kept the appearance of calm detachment after the shock of a sudden death when there were decisions to be made, tasks to be completed, and when others you loved were looking to you for comfort and guidance. But, stoicism, tearless composure, and remarkable organizing skills are not the qualities you must exercise as you move on past the initial shock of grief to accept the emotional demands of your loss. You can't always remain silent and brave behind a veil of quiet strength. To fully acknowledge the wrenching, soul-tearing pain of grief requires a special courage. It's this courage and openness to being vulnerable that will enable you to move toward the other shore of grief.

CHOOSE SUFFERING—THE BETTER CHOICE

Seek to find the words that works for you. If you feel "mad as hell," say so. My husband's references to feelings of "deep sadness" suggest the very depths of pain the soul can know. It's worth the search to face your pain, for if you fail to do so, the pain can eventually claim you. If you do not resolve your anger, it may be displaced and directed at innocent friends and family members. Unrelenting guilt can lead to destructive acts of self punishment. Sorrow ignored goes underground and waits for a later time when it surfaces more intense than ever. When these feelings are "banned", you become their prisoner and get stuck in the grief process. Marcel Proust, a French author, reminds us that "We are healed of suffering only by experiencing it to the fullest."

In the movie *Shadowlands*, C.S. Lewis compares his reaction to his mother's death, when he was a boy and his pain at her loss was never acknowledged, to his reaction years later at the loss of his wife. He observes, "The boy chose safety; the man chose suffering." The safety in denying pain did not work; it was his choice as an adult to endure suffering that ultimately healed him of both losses. Don't be afraid to choose suffering, for this is the healthiest path to recovery.

THE SURPRISING SECOND WISH

My second wish during the weeks after our son's death was that the wrenching, all consuming pain would go away. One morning as I was taking a vitamin, I thought how wonderful it would be if there was a pill like this that would make the anguish and missing just go away. For a crazy few seconds I thought of calculating how many pills I would require for the rest of my life. I then had a true appreciation for the temptation which drugs and alcohol offer to alleviate such suffering.

And, then, a strange thought crossed my mind, "What would it be like to be totally pain free now as if it hadn't happened, as if it didn't matter or have any value?" I pondered what the pain free miracle would say about me, about the importance of Eric, about loving him and being his mother. I still don't have any grand resolutions to these "ponderings." But I rephrased my wish . . . "Please," I prayed, "just let it get better." And it did.

CHAPTER 4

THE STRESSES IN SPECIFIC LOSSES

Working with bereavement groups for more than a dozen years has helped me appreciate the main reactions and stresses in different losses, and the many concerns that are specific for each one. These highlights of many voices from our groups may also speak for you.

THE LOSS OF A PARENT

In many ways this is the most challenging loss, for this has been the longest relationship in our lives, since our very beginning. At different developmental stages in our lives, we experience the healthy, normal stresses which inevitably bring conflict, anger, resentment, guilt. Even as infants there was the need for unconditional love yet anger that we were so needy. One distraught woman wailed when telling of the death of her second parent, "I'm nobody's little girl any more." She had suddenly discovered she was now an orphan. When a parent dies, we tend to dredge up all our childhood failures and misdemeanors, real or imagined. These can become a burden for us the rest of our lives if we lose perspective. If their recent situation has taxed our energies and patience, we feel guilty that we didn't handle it better. Although parents may be gone, sibling rivalry can be stronger than ever at this time. Perhaps we still want to affirm, "I was the favorite, I did the most." The family may have faced difficult medical decisions. Often there's a difference of opinion about funeral arrangements, division of personal effects, and how to do the holidays now.

There can be worry about the surviving parent who may not be able to function independently at this time. But, if one such parent, usually the father, starts dating, the thought of him remarrying can seem an effrontery to the memory of their mother. There's sadness that our children are now denied the joys and privileges only grandparents can bestow, sadness that Mom won't see the new generation grow, flourish, and pass on the family traditions. Parents were the people who were always there to take your side, trust your better motives, and provide the reassurance, advice, and help that only a parent can. We're never too old to need or want this.

SHOE POLISH AND ACUTE GRIEF

My mother's death was an enormous shock and heartache for me. It happened when we had first moved to Maryland and had two children under two years. We were renting a pretty nice apartment in a large apartment complex until we could arrange to buy or build a house. At that time apartments all had asphalt tile floors, edged all around by black tile baseboards that readily showed scuffing and other marks.

My husband was on a business trip when I got the totally unexpected and horrifying news that my mother in Minnesota was dying of cancer. As my husband made immediate arrangements to return home, I got ready to leave for Minnesota. Here's how I prepared for the sad journey.

The evening I heard the news, still reeling from shock, I went out and bought a dozen bottles of liquid black shoe polish with sponge applicators. During the LONG night, on my hands and knees, I meticulously painted every inch of baseboard with the shoe polish. The next day the apartment looked very bright and new; I looked old and worn and sore. But, the activity got me through the night, and that's what mattered.

CHILD LOSS

Parents were invented to keep children safe. That's what we do. And, when all our love, care, and worry can't do this, it's a travesty, a crime against creation itself. We are supposed to die first, and when the natural order of the universe is reversed, the glue that sustains the very fabric of our lives dissolves. A month after Eric's death, I was baby sitting with my first grandchild, Kirk, who was almost two. It was amazing how old patterns of vigilance emerged as I watched him play. Since the sidewalks in front of my daughter's home were noticeably uneven in places from encroaching tree roots. I followed closely behind his bursts of toddler sprinting to be sure I'd catch him if he tripped. Suddenly a terrible realization slammed into my mind. "Oh, dear God," I thought, "all the years I monitored my children's faltering steps, all the times I've diligently and protectively watched my own toddler Eric running and jumping—and I couldn't save the nineteen year old boy from the fatal misstep. All that watching, all the worrying, all that caution, and I couldn't rescue him when it was a matter of life and death." The unfairness of it, the horrendous irony suddenly made me so weak I had to sit down on the curb gasping for breath and controlling the sudden nausea. The pain was so visceral I wished that parenthood had never been invented. It was a time when I nearly went under, so powerful were the waves of despair. But, I didn't. I still kept a watchful eye on my young charge with his boundless energy.

Marriages Beware

This can be a perilous time for marriages. An alarming number of divorces occur in the year following the death of a child. If the marriage has been unstable before, if there's been difficulty communicating, if there's been disagreements about child raising, or if one parent already has emotional difficulties, the couple might need help. If so, they should get marriage counseling sooner rather than later. They shouldn't wait this one out.

REMEMBER, WE ALL HANDLE OUR GRIEF DIFFERENTLY

Many couples have difficulty recognizing and adjusting to the reality that men grieve differently than women. Social expectations and years of conditioning dictate that men should be in control, take change, "do something" at this traumatic time when they are most vulnerable themselves. Men may find their only solace in work, in physical activity when women need to talk and go over the story again and again. Or it could be reversed: the man needs to grieve outwardly and the woman starts spring housecleaning in February. One parent might be depressed and require solitude while the other may crave activities or projects to keep the family together. They may be grieving on different schedules. She might be moving into phase two where she needs to talk about and analyze her troublesome feelings, whereas he may still be in shock, unable to accept the reality of such a loss. A father in one of our groups complained that his wife just wanted to watch family videos of their daughter who had recently been killed in an accident, but he couldn't stand seeing her picture and would have to leave the house at these times. At a time of such wrenching crisis, it's hard to find necessary reserves of patience. If nothing else works, just honor each other's right to find his own swimming stroke or to just tread water at times. Trust that the anger and pain won't be there forever. And if you use the lifelines of reliable outside support, things can get better.

Worry About the Other Children

Then there's the awful worry about the other children, knowing we can't spare them from their anguish, knowing we can't do anything to make this hurt go away. My husband and I chose to have four children in six years. One of our major parental goals was to do all we could to ensure our kids would grow up to be good friends when they reached their teenage years, as well as just siblings. This doesn't automatically happen in many families. I encouraged the older ones, Katrina and Karl to have their own friends and activities and tried to see that the younger ones didn't interfere with their independent pursuits. It was our responsibility as the parents to discipline if a child did something wrong or dangerous. They just had to keep each other safe and enjoy one another.

And, for the most part, they did have fun together. Of course it wasn't perfect, especially when they were young. We dealt with the usual competitiveness, the "It's my turn to sit by the car window," "You always give her . . . ." and "I never get a chance" scenarios. But, as the children became adult teenagers, all the good had come back. They were close friends and enjoyed each other's company more than that of other friends. We had succeeded in our big plan. Interestingly enough, it was Eric who became the keystone for their renewed siblinghood. The summer before his accident, Eric decided to organize his own sibling family reunion. Karl and Greta had summer jobs at Rehoboth Beach, about a three hours' drive away, and Katrina was living in Baltimore with her husband and year old baby. But, Eric was determined that his siblings needed to get together. His enthusiasm was infectious. The beach workers managed somehow to get a Sunday off from jobs, and Katrina graciously agreed to be the hostess. My husband and I were invited, but declined, so they would have their own time together. It was indeed a wonderful day, a day Eric made possible; they decided it should be an annual summer tradition from then on.

But, of course, a year later they were gathered for his memorial service, stunned. The friendship and closeness our children had, just as we had always wanted it to be, made it that much more difficult when he died. The greatest pain I have ever known next to Eric's death is the pain of knowing how dreadful it is for them. We were a family of six, with two sons and two daughters. It was perfectly balanced. Eric's death changed it all; Greta suddenly became the youngest, the twenty-two year old "baby" of the family. Karl was suddenly the only son; the girls had just one brother. I was a mother of four, with three children. Every parent I counsel tearfully and desperately asks, "What do I say when people ask me how many children I have?" I still don't have a comfortable answer for such a natural innocent question that still makes me feel "zero at the bone."

WHEN A CHILD DIES BEFORE HE HAS A CHANCE TO LIVE

People may assume that child loss doesn't include miscarriage or infant death. Believe me, those who have suffered such sad losses know better. Before a child is born, parents have their hopes, their expectations, their visions and dreams of how their lives will be with their new family. "This is how we'll handle Santa Claus and Christmas. But for now we'll have a real excuse to visit the zoo, to make the trip to Disney World." When a child dies at birth, all these dreams are shattered; they never had a chance. And, to make it even worse, there hasn't even been time for others to know him and share his history. Except for a few sonograms, there are no pictures to chronicle the sacred milestones in that precious life. Friends and family can't say, "Remember how cute she was when . . ." or "I remember how proud we were when he." And because they didn't know him, because he didn't live that long, the enormity of his loss is easily discounted by others. It is the loneliest grief of all. For the pain is never measured by the length of a child's life.

When an adult dies in the fullness of time, it's reasonable to say we are primarily grieving for ourselves, not for them. But this isn't the whole story when a child dies. We legitimately grieve for what they have been denied, the chance to savor their full share of the joys and challenges of life. I grieve for the future our son will never experience, the future unfulfilled promise of his life. Finally, we all grieve for the talents, the love, the gifts the world was denied by the death of these children. *And, oh, we miss them so.*

DEATH OF A SPOUSE

"I don't belong to anyone anymore. I'm not special to anyone," an acquaintance observed plaintively as she tried to figure out the really hardest part of being widowed, a wrenching loneliness. My friend continued, "You know, Jack had lots of interests and activities and things he'd talk about that were not my interests particularly, but he'd still bring this part of himself into our lives, and now I don't have that part either. It's as if those parts of him have been cut out."

A friend, referring to the trauma she experienced after a bitter divorce spoke with insight and authority when she said, "When I got my divorce it was just like a death. It's like you're on this little island, alone, your own island." What an apt comparison for the sense of utter separation that makes so many feel forever stranded and alone.

Several years ago, a favorite television show was the *Mary Tyler Moore Show* about a gorgeous, young, vibrant and skinny young girl who moves to Minneapolis to start her life in broadcasting. The opening of each episode shows her standing in the middle of a busy city intersection joyously tossing her cute little hat into the air; in the background, we hear the cheerful, thematic chorus, "You're Gonna Make It On Your Own." Those who are newly widowed don't feel so hopeful about making it on their own. Their future seems uncertain. At this time of great crisis, widows must quickly adjust to and cope with many demands: handling insurance, making decisions, coping with loss of income or the necessity to get back in the job market, handling housekeeping chores and shopping or yard duty, and the challenge of suddenly becoming a single parent under the most wretched conditions.

You miss most the companionship in sharing the daily, routine events in your lives. Deciding what to fix for dinner, talking about work, sharing concerns for their family, even arguing about differing political views; the activities we take so for granted are suddenly just not there. No matter how busy and filled the days are, there's always the searing reminder— when you must at last return, and open the door to an empty house—that he's not there, and won't be returning. And, it's not just the sex. It's the holding, the touching, the hugs, the just being there.

All too often a widow is abruptly dropped from the social circle of couples with whom "they" have been so comfortable. It seems as if she has no dimension or status in her own right. Other wives may consider her a threat to their marriages and be more concerned for protecting themselves than supporting her. At the time she needs their comfort and affirmation most, they abandon her. Still all must change from being part of a "we" to being an "I." A friend explained her anger at having to declare a new, unwanted identity when she provides personal information on business forms. "I refuse to check the box marked single," she said. "I put a big "W" in it."

But, even if you don't feel "like a single person", you must cope with it all, the work, the unfairness, the questions, the fears without the help and love of your spouse, the person with whom you'd shared everything. At the time of Eric's death, despite the numbness and confusion, I realized that I had the luxury of grieving without worrying about the decisions and responsibilities shouldered by my husband. Since then I've had unparalleled respect and admiration for widows who miraculously cope with the demands of a new world while grieving such a terrible loss, while missing their loved one so.

SUICIDE

As I was starting this book, I learned of two suicides, and was reminded of several other such tragedies I had known of in the past, losses that happen probably far more often than we know. There's the added sorrow that their loved one resorted to such a final, irrevocable act to solve problems or cope with depression. How terrible that they couldn't use our concern, and resources to receive solace. "What was going through his mind? Why did this happen now? Why didn't I do something?", questions that will forever haunt us. There is no loss where guilt is harder to assuage. Surely we could have, "should have done something," we torture ourselves. But, although a particular event or depressive episode might have triggered the final act, it was not the whole cause. Complex factors over a period of several years have played a part, factors over which we probably had no control.

The suicide was their decision, their choice, and we are not responsible for that. Even trained counselors are often powerless to predict, much less control, a client's suicidal impulses. We can't be mind readers. We have such limited control over the destinies our loved ones choose. With other types of death, we gain some comfort by talking about the death, telling the story over and over. People then respond, ask questions, and we can tell it again and talk about the terrible feelings. But often the survivors of suicide don't wish to talk about the death, perhaps somehow feeling ashamed, and they retreat behind a veil of secrecy. Although they need sympathy for their loss, they don't want to nor should they have to provide details. They want to suffer in silence. Suffering in silence can exact a terrible price. It's hard to persuade many survivors that they are not alone; lifeboats of fellow sufferers are out there to guide them to shore. They are the special support groups for suicide survivors (see p. 92).

VIOLENT DEATH

A MAN SHOT DOWN
A CHILD ABDUCTED, HER MURDERED BODY FOUND LATER
A CHILD MISSING AND NEVER FOUND
A WOMAN RAPED BY A STRANGER AND THEN MURDERED
A HUSBAND REPORTS EARLY TO HIS JOB AT THE WORLD TRADE
    CENTER ON SEPTEMBER 11.
STUDENT GOES ON SHOOTING SPREE IN LOCAL HIGH SCHOOL
Although these horrors are beyond comprehension, beyond any civilized reasoning, they are reality. I can't imagine the unending rage and anguish their loved ones must live with day by day. I can only acknowledge that such atrocities exist. And I must confess I don't have adequate words of comfort to offer. This is when we are beyond the "telling of it" and can only find tears.

BUT I WONDER . . . .

After he doesn't come home,
After the hours or days or weeks of waiting,
After the search,
After the again waiting,
After the body is found,
After the again waiting,
After the arrest,

After the long trial,
After the sentencing,
After the appeals,
After the press demands and interviews,
After the punishment,
After justice,
What happens now?
Is it ever over?
Or must we now resume the lonely business
Of grieving?

Several years ago, I was asked by a minister acquaintance who knew of my training in pastoral counseling if I'd lead a bereavement group at his church while he sat in as a co-leader to observe. "I've got several ladies in my church who have suffered terrible losses and they need help badly."

Boy, was he right. He was pastor of a middle class all black congregation in a residential area in Washington, D.C. We met for six Saturday mornings. Nowhere could I have learned more about courage and strength in the face of violent death. I forget many details, but there were eight women in this gathering; most had lost a beloved husband or son in a violent encounter. This was reality.

One, a young mother of two told how her husband, a D.C. police officer had been shot on Christmas Eve. She had decided to start a tradition of holding an open house for neighbors and his fellow officers from then on Christmas Eve. But she couldn't decide to wash his soft flannel shirt, the one she kept near her pillow every night. "I'm afraid I'll wash his special smell out of it, and that's all I have left."

One lady was a grandmother who had been raising her fifteen year old grandson while her daughter was in a drug rehab program. She'd arranged for him to get special work training at a separate school. As a cousin was driving him to school, he'd been shot to death in a random drive-by shooting.

Another lady's son in his early twenties had been found drowned in the Potomac River. She knew it was no accident. She was sure he had been murdered by some neighborhood gang. She knew there was nothing she could safely do about it.

As they recited their stories of horror, I just wept, but they forgave my professional lapse and tried to comfort *me*! After that first session, we proceeded with the established bereavement format. The sessions went so well, an accomplishment that was a great satisfaction and comfort to me.

There's more to this story, but you'll have to read about it in chapter 8 "Good News."

COMPETING WITH 9/11 AND HURRICANE KATRINA

What about the incomprehensible global disasters that claim thousands and thousands of lives, each one part of some family and community structure that suffers as much as we? In the face of such unbelievable circumstances when entire family systems are destroyed, how dare we complain that our grief at the loss of just one person is unbearable? The answer for me is . . . we're not competing. It's not about mere numbers; it's beyond mathematics. But it's not beyond the pain and everyone's inalienable right to grieve and be comforted.

ALL LOSSES HURT ONE HUNDRED PERCENT AND COUNTING

All losses matter, not just the big four I've emphasized here. When a friend dies, we lose a special confidant, a keeper of secrets, a chosen sister or brother. Despite in-law jokes, these relationships can be as strong and fulfilling as those with our own parents. Grieving the loss of a child's fiancé can be as wrenching as surviving the loss of one's own child. And our pets, who love us unconditionally, enthusiastically, and publicly, deserve their full measure of mourning. They only worry about pleasing us, not what others think. They can be our quiet trusted companion and solace. They forgive more generously and readily than many adults. Is it any wonder their death can leave a void no person can fill?

People often promote a hierarchy of grief from the "worst loss" on down the line. I have had too many broken-hearted grievers apologize because they are so sad about the death of an elderly parent when "I know nothing can compare with the loss of a child." Despite their kindness, they have a false understanding about pain. It's the experience, the pain of loss that matters. All losses hurt a hundred percent. Each and every loss deserves the full measure of our grief and tears. Don't let anyone tell you otherwise.

CHAPTER 5

GRIEVING THE DEATH OF THE UNLOVING
GRIEVING THE DEATH OF THE RECKLESS

Many books and articles are written about grieving the death of a loved one. However, I haven't seen any guidelines for grieving the death of an unloving or unloved one. I've seen little on grieving the deaths of loved ones whose reckless or irresponsible behavior led to their deaths. In these situations we also struggle with the unkindest thoughts of all. In an ideal world, blighted relationships wouldn't exist, but in reality they do exist and demand attention if we are ever going to get better.

We can accept the requirements of adjusting to the normal ambivalances that are natural in all relationships. Those we love most, who love us best have weaknesses, hurt us, let us down at times, or have irritating habits that grate on our nerves. After all, that's to be expected in even the closest relationships. Our responsibility is not to forge a mantle of perfection on a relationship that's ended by death, but to honestly, even humorously, grieve for the true person, with the good and bad mixed together.

WHEN THE MEMORIES AREN'T GOOD

But what about the other times when it's been mostly bad, when there are a shortage of thoughts and memories to soften the harsh reality that this person I needed to love me didn't love me. What about the times when the shadow side is all there is?

"ROSEANNE" AND THE NUTSHELL VERSION

In one episode of the television comedy show "Roseanne," her father has just died. Apparently he had been unfaithful, leaving his wife to marry a younger woman; and obviously he had not been a great father to his two girls; the anger and bitterness is quite apparent in the opening scenes as the family prepares to attend his funeral. Finally, at the end of the episode, Roseanne is alone in the mortuary room. She takes a piece of paper out of her pocket and proceeds to read a carefully prepared list of grievances to her father's flower bedecked casket. It is a cold recitation in a sad monotone. It was something like this.

"I hate that you left us . . . ."

"I hate that you never were there . . . ."

"I hate that you played around and got another girl friend and left Mom."

"I hate it that we have to take care of her, this crazy woman . . . ."

After this angry and painful recitation, she is very quiet for a few minutes. Then, dropping the crumpled list on the floor, she announces in a calmer voice . . . .

"I forgive you, so I can go on with my life."

"I forgive myself for being so angry and hating you so."

As she leaves the viewing room, she quickly glances back and quickly whispers, almost as an afterthought . . .

"I guess I got some of your sense of humor. Love ya. Bye."

Her sad monologue seems to represent this painful grief reaction in a nutshell. Unfortunately in real life it's not completed in a half hour show.

However, the feelings in that show mirrored the excruciating grief I knew when my father died. He traveled extensively when we were growing up, often accepting professorships at various universities in the country: he was seldom home. When he was home, he was distant, unapproachable, and uncomfortable with family relationships and responsibilities. He never talked to us. He was also an alcoholic, often in some stage of intoxication and although never physically abusive, his violent rants and ravings were terrifying.

So, when he battled cancer ten years after my mother's death, I was sorry but hardly expected the emotional trauma and heartache I'd known during her illness. News of his death came one afternoon when I was home alone. To my surprise and horror I was swamped with an emotion beyond the boundaries of anger. My white hot rage could have sparked a forest fire. Many of us were taught that we must never speak ill of the dead. But in reality, if we stifle all the negative feelings or anger about someone who has died, we hinder our recovery from grief. Fortunately, my instincts told me this was not the time to "stifle."

"Damn you," I screamed to my deceased Dad in our empty living room, "how dare you die without ever being there for me, without ever saying you were proud of me, without ever noticing how desperately I tried to please you, without ever saying you loved me. How dare you die leaving me only memories of terror, of anxious days and uneasy encounters". I recalled sitting with my high school graduation class on the stage cringing with embarrassment when my father arrived under the influence half way through the ceremony and stumbled down the auditorium aisle looking for his seat. My pre-wedding jitters were worsened by my unspoken fear that the same thing would happen at my wedding. Searching desperately for the "good times," for signs that it wasn't as bad as I remembered, failed. I was grieving the death of an unloving parent.

Later, I reflected on the reason for the unbridled outburst and was able to help myself figure out what was going on. I wasn't grieving his death; I was grieving the fact that I had nothing to grieve, nothing good to miss. I was grieving the final knowledge that even if I had still harbored fantasies that he would change, that I would merit his love, there was absolutely no chance now of their being fulfilled. The words, the touch, the affirmation so needed would never be there. At the same time I was angry at myself for the years of futile hopes and unrealistic expectations. Why wasn't I smart enough to bury those before he died?. Why was I such a pitifully slow learner?

And then, just as suddenly, I was no longer frightened by the enormity of my fury, for I understood it, I had explained it to myself, and it made sense. Eventually the anger and hate faded to sadness, a deep sadness for us both. I had learned that we don't need to make the real people in our lives into "heroes" to honorably mourn them. I had learned that we are also required to struggle and grieve a separate death when we grieve the love that never was.

I recovered because I ignored the unspoken "rule" forbidding me to say anything that wasn't "nice." I said the bad things out loud to my husband and trusted friends. You don't have to go on talk shows or write a *Mommy Dearest* ©, but you must find the words to say what you feel, to yourself and to a confidant, trusting that doing so will help you cope with the pain and get better.

CAN FORGIVENESS BE PART OF THIS?

After the anger and the tears, don't forget that forgiveness is always an option. Years ago I counseled a young woman who had endured a destructive relationship. I don't recall details, but I think her husband had kicked her, causing her to lose their child. There was a lot of wretched stuff there. But I will never forget one session that had been particularly intense and tearful. As she left the room, she turned around and in a sad, resigned "little girl" voice very quietly stated, "I guess forgiveness will be there, down the line."

Her sad acceptance seemed very wise. She wasn't talking about reconciling or tolerating the marriage any longer. But, she had realized that "down the line" if she was going to make a new life for herself, she would need to find the place for forgiveness. Down the line, we too can strive to just let the bad things go. The dead who have injured us have done enough damage. We need not allow them any more opportunities to make us weep.

ABOUT OUR "UNMENTIONABLES": THE WORDS WE DARE NOT SPEAK

Many thoughts besides the unkind ones about an unloving person may also cross your mind, thoughts that seem negative, even unmentionable. Like feelings, your thoughts, in themselves, do not make you a degenerate, evil person. Actually, these can be helpful because examining and talking about them can lead to a better understanding of what's going on in your heart and mind.

Here's nine honest, understandable "non-bad" thoughts that are all too often hidden in shame, where they fester for years and cast a powerful pall over our lives.

1. I wish my other parent or sibling had died instead.
2. I'm free. Thank God almighty, I'm free at last.

3. I'm glad she's dead.
4. I loved him so, but I hate him for dying so soon.
5. I'm going crazy.
6. I wish I were dead.
7. Actually, I'm happier now than before she died.
8. If I stop feeling bad, if I get better, I'll forget him.
9. If I have a good time, I'm being unfaithful.

These thoughts make sense. You may have your own to add. Instead of understanding them, we cover them up with the BIG "G". Now, you know better.

WHEN THEY BRING IT ON THEMSELVES: WAITING FOR THE OTHER SHOE TO DROP

There's a special category of heartbreaking refrains that may go like this:

"He wouldn't give up smoking. We told him how bad it was but he just wouldn't listen."

"He was such a wild kid, always driving recklessly. We tried everything, but he thought he was indestructible. He just wouldn't listen."

"Her blood pressure and cholesterol were so high. The doctor even warned her, but we just couldn't get her to pay attention."

"She simply didn't believe in mammograms. We couldn't persuade her how important they were."

"He had such a battle with drugs. Despite all the rehab programs we arranged, he didn't stop and he got an overdose. He just wouldn't let us help."

"He knew as well as anyone about the precautions people must take to avoid getting AIDS. But he didn't take them seriously enough no matter how much we worried."

"She sort of bragged that she was too busy to always monitor her sugar levels and worry about her insulin intake. She just wouldn't take our worry for her diabetes seriously."

"No matter what we said or tried to do, he'd drink and drive. We knew this would happen some day, but he just wouldn't believe it."

These are just a few of many scenarios, I'm sure. What about these times when despite all your pleas and efforts, someone's actions and behavior are a major contributor to his death? Worse yet, when they cause someone else's death too? What about the times they bring it on themselves? These deaths too bring their own brand of hurt and anger that can't be ignored. We're so tempted to say, "If he really loved me, he would have . . . ." or "If she really cared about us, she wouldn't have . . .," thoughts that make the loss, the guilt, and the anger even more cruel. "If only," we despair, "he'd just have had a really close call while tailgating, . . . and then he'd have had a second chance. Surely then he would have reformed and finally listened to us." Part of us screams, "You fool, why were you too stubborn to listen?" And the sadness following a death that maybe didn't have to happen is immeasurable. There's not even the comfort of having the final word, "I told you so."

But, it finally *did* happen. You might have lived with this person for years, a lifetime in fear for his health, with the gut hurting foreboding and terrible knowing that his behavior would ultimately "catch up with him." And, after all the years, years of frustration coping with his indifference to our pleas and worries, sure enough, it finally did happen. The wearisome suspense is finally lifted to be replaced by understandable rage, and, yes, even the crucifying guilt that we in some way had the power to change them, and failed. However, if the rage, helpless fury, and preposterous guilt keep building up inside you, there won't be any chance to get better. Tell *someone* how you really feel; tell a friend, tell God, tell your dog, throw pillows against the wall, take a walk in the woods and smash some branches, write in your journal or write a letter to this person whose indifference to your worries has caused you such grief. Just get it out in the open so your heart can heal.

SECOND THOUGHTS

I'd like to offer three thoughts for your consideration, for you to think about after you've screamed and cussed and cried.

1. We can't possibly know what really goes on in someone else's heart and mind. They probably did do the best they could to conquer an addiction or change potentially dangerous behavior. We didn't know of the many private struggles they may have waged, or the

disappointment they had when they failed. We only saw their weakness and our despair. They may have desperately tried to change; perhaps we owe them at last the benefit of the doubt.

2. We want to believe that our love is perfect enough to enable a loved one to change, to save himself. But, perhaps "perfect love" doesn't make those we love perfect; it perhaps enables us to love them, even with their imperfections.

3. We were not responsible for their behavior or their choices. We did the best we could; we tried, but our power was limited by their weakness, by the struggles they couldn't overcome. Even blaming them wears off after a long time, and we're left with the terribly sad needless tragedy of it all.

THEIRS ARE DEATHS WORTH MOURNING

No matter the cause, no matter the circumstances, we grieve just as deeply for our reckless loved ones as any other loss. It matters not, finally, how or why they died. It only matters that they are our dear ones who are lost, and missed. They should be mourned. We should be comforted.

CHAPTER 6

COPING WITH CHILDREN, HOLIDAYS, AND THE "WHY?" OF IT ALL

The second "phase" of grief seems to go on forever and forever. We are seldom given the luxury of just coping with our private struggle and overpowering feelings. Other responsibilities and decisions will be part of our lives and must have our attention. For example, three struggles emerge in almost every grief situation. We always have to cope with them before we're ready, but they can bludgeon their way into our sorrow demanding our immediate attention. What about the children? How are we going to survive the holidays and anniversaries? Why, why did this have to happen to us?

AND WE SHALL HAVE CINNAMON TOAST

Almost everyone is concerned for the children in a family when there is such upheaval. Worry about your child at the time you're so unsure and unhappy can make the confusion and pain worse. I'm offering a few general guidelines that may help.

1. Attention must be paid to ways younger children in the family understand what has happened. In the chaos surrounding death, they are so easily ignored. However, sensitive adults must repeatedly ask young children to tell them, "What happened when Daddy died" or "why did Aunt Jane die?" It's so important to check their perceptions and understandings of what happened. Many may secretly fear that the favorite child in their family died, and this survivor guilt is reinforced by their parents' distraction and irritability at this time.

In situations where there's been a very traumatic or violent death, locate a child psychologist or counselor who can help a younger child by speaking his language through toys, drawings, playing, by talking about the "good and the bad guys," and who is familiar with the scary parts of a child's world.

2. Children sense what's going on. They feel the tension and may suspect there's some secret, something really bad happening, possibly something they caused. So, they need to be included in appropriate ways. Tell them the truth; this is no time for euphemisms. Daddy has not "gone," he is not "asleep", he is dead. When people die they can't come back. A child can be included in services if someone explains what is going on, how people may be very sad and tearful, and helps him to anticipate what will happen. Surprisingly enough, many find it helpful and appropriate for young children to attend a viewing. If his hand is safely and firmly held by a trusted, loving adult, and again the child is prepared for what will happen, this experience can help him grasp the finality of death. Of course, you don't force a child to attend any funeral activity if he's so anxious he refuses.

3. Reassure a child that he will be loved and cared for by adults, by you. You will still be here loving and caring for him. A newly widowed young mother was horrified that her seven year old son's first response to news of his father's death was to wail, "But, who's going to drive me to soccer practice?" He wasn't unfeeling, he just needed immediate reassurance that his world wasn't going to just disappear, too. This was the advice given by mental health professionals to parents reeling from the utter devastation in their own lives after hurricane Katrina. Do all you can to provide a sense of security and continuity, not so easy to do when your own world is crumbling. Yet maintain as much as possible your normal "discipline" expectations which in themselves provide a reassurance that things aren't out of control. Keep reassuring him that things will be all right. "When the stores are open, we'll be able to get bread and you shall have cinnamon toast."

4. Repeatedly let your child know he is in no way to blame or responsible for the death. Young children experience "magical thinking" which means they believe their bad thoughts have the power to cause certain things to happen. "Maybe Mom died because I didn't clean my room and came home late." "Maybe my baby sister died because I wished

she'd go away and never come back." Explain that we all have had times when we've been angry or had unhappy thoughts about the person who died, but these didn't have anything to do with it. Let him know that thoughts don't make him bad or cause bad things to happen.

5. Although a child needs stability and security, children also need to learn that grieving hurts and makes us sad. Of course, prolonged outbursts could frighten anyone, but your child needs to see you cry and hear you talk about your sadness, about the missing. He needs the permission you model to go ahead and grieve his loss, too. Many years ago, a young mother who was a friend of my daughter's died of cancer, a tragedy that was talked about in Katrina's family. About two weeks later, Katrina's five year old son came up to her suddenly and asked, "If I died, Mom, would you miss me?" I'm amazed at the calm, wonderful answer she gave. First she reassured him that children his age don't usually get cancer, that he was safe and in no danger of dying. Then, she said, "Honey, you remember that my younger brother, your Uncle Eric, died before you were born. Well, I loved him very much and when he died, I cried every day for a year, then every week for a year, and then every month for a year, and then I got better. It would be like that if anything happened to you." She let him know that his life mattered, that he would be mourned. She let him know that the sadness of missing someone who has died is something to cry about, to cry about for a long time. And, she let him know that it wouldn't stay so bad, that it would get better. It made sense and, greatly reassured, her child returned to his play.

6. Puppets help. I personally didn't work with children's bereavement groups our Silver Spring hospice sponsored, but such groups serve a real need in a compassionate and creative way. There's a project our children's group devised that may be helpful for you. Each child makes a very simple sock puppet and draws a sad or worried face on his special creation. Whenever he feels sad or worried about the death he is grieving, he places the sad-faced puppet on the pillow of the adult he'd like to talk to. The child has a simple way to let people know when he needs to talk, and adults know when they can be most helpful. I think it's a super idea for children. And, I wonder what it would be like if we could all have our own puppets to help us ask for help.

HOLIDAY AND ANNIVERSARY HORRORS

The first holiday, birthday, and anniversaries after a loss are anticipated with such dread and fear that we're sometimes surprised when the day finally comes and goes and we find we got through it better than we ever thought possible. Our son died on June 13, and our wedding anniversary was exactly one week later. By July first I was beginning to panic about how we'd manage Christmas. I was pretty sure the unbearable pain of his birthday in March would surely kill us so I kinda figured we wouldn't be around to have to worry about the first anniversary of his death. But, I was still around and had to face it.

THE ANNIVERSARY LETTERS

I worried about our other children knowing how difficult this would be for them. So, about three weeks before the dreaded anniversary, I started making detailed lists of all the things each child had done and accomplished in the past impossible year. I noted all their kindnesses to us, all they had done to help with Christmas, all they had accomplished in their jobs and for their families. Actually, I had a pretty impressive list for each; just focusing on that project lifted my spirits. Then, I wrote each of my children a personal letter to be opened on June 13. I referred only briefly to this being the anniversary of their brother's death, simply acknowledging how terrible the year had been. I reminded each that one reason Eric had been so special and wonderful was because of the love, nurturing, and affirmation he had received from her/him, and what an important contribution he had made to his brother' s life. Then, I simply went through my catalogue of all this child had done during the past year, all the loving he had shown, all the challenges he had faced, all that he had accomplished. I said how proud I was, how much we parents celebrated all he had become during the crucible of grief. Mailing those letters helped me get past the dreaded day. It felt good because I knew that was exactly what Eric would have wanted.

CAN'T WE SKIP THE HOLIDAYS THIS YEAR?

No matter when the death occurred, people in our groups are almost immediately scared about the holidays, even if Christmas, or Passover, or

Eid al Fitr, is ten months away. You don't have to make these first holidays perfect, like they used to be. During this first terrible year, you just need to get through these wretched days to the next day on the calendar. However, you shouldn't stay frozen and let them just "happen" either. You have to figure out what's going to work for you. You have to take charge here. The crucial point is to plan something, get some battle strategy in place.

Many people in our groups needed to keep holiday traditions the way they were; the comfort of familiar rituals helped. Just as many, however, needed to change the usual routine or do something entirely different. Taking a vacation to warm climates for Christmas enabled many to get through it. We celebrated Christmas that first year by adopting an entirely different schedule for our activities. Our daughter Greta volunteered to take the night shift at the hospital where she was nursing. She decided it was going to be a painful night anyhow, so she might as well give other nurses a chance to be home. Consequently, her work schedule actually helped us make changes in our routine. I couldn't bear going to the midnight service at our own church, so we attended an early informal service at another church, which had less emotional associations. After this service we had a simple dinner at a restaurant in time for Greta to get ready for her late shift. It was a happy, festive meal, a good choice although we had never eaten out on Christmas Eve before and have never done so since. But it got us through that evening, and that's what mattered most. Since Greta had worked all night, we opened our presents much later and had a late afternoon Christmas dinner. However, that year we tried out all new recipes because we couldn't bear the family traditional meal with Eric's favorite apple jelly sauce. Yet the following year, we went back to the old, usual pattern, apple jelly sauce and all.*

Anniversaries and birthdays are brutal. Again, you just need to get to the next day. Again it's important to plan what you are going to do or not do. Find your own plan; you don't need to do what others do. Maybe your plan is to be alone, to cry, to be sad, to look at pictures and special mementoes. That's a good plan if it's comfortable for you. You may need to be busy and undertake a project like cleaning out the basement or yard work. I can see the value of tackling some distasteful, unpleasant task that must be done. If it's going to be a miserable day, you might as well make good use of it.

How sad it is that these joyous occasions are now tinged with longing and missing. The truth is that they will never be the same. But the truth is also that the pain changes, and these days don't stay frozen in overwhelming grief forever. And, you have some say about getting through. A holiday gift or donation to a cause or project you know your loved one would enthusiastically endorse can help. We adopted this plan a few years ago. It helps us to decide on these gift choices when we're denied the opportunity to give a present to the one we miss so at this time.

*ERIC'S FAVORITE APPLE JELLY SAUCE FOR HOLIDAY HAM OR LIMA BEANS

1 large glass apple jelly, 1/4 teaspoon cinnamon, 2 teaspoons vinegar
1 teaspoon dry mustard, ½ teaspoon cloves

Bring jelly and spices to a boil; then put into a pitcher and serve hot. This keeps for weeks in the refrigerator and is also good served cold on ham sandwiches.

AND HOW DOES GOD FIT INTO THIS?

We harbor the faith that surely love, goodness, and sacrifice, will keep a loved one safe or bring him back from the brink of death. We want to believe that the good ones, those who make the world a better place, will be protected and survive. But to our dismay, it doesn't always happen this way. A negligent driver may get off with a warning or token jail sentence, while a husband, father, and provider has been killed without the courtesy of a second chance. Life is not fair. And so we wrestle with the biggie, the question that can bring anger as well as solace, "Where does God fit into this?" First of all, you don't have to have to figure it all out and have answers immediately. The Bible story of Job shows that disasters will shake the best of us for a while, and Jesus himself, as he was being crucified, perhaps had a moment of doubt, of terror that possibly God had forsaken him. You too can expect a few dark nights of the soul without your faith being in total jeopardy.

But, the religious and philosophical quest for answers, for a perspective on the "big picture" can invade and persist, the big issues theologians and philosophers have wrestled with since the beginning of time. It is unfair to expect yourself to "get the answer down pat" at this particular time of sudden crisis when the pain and despair claim all your energy. So, don't force this added burden on yourself now if to do so confuses you, enrages you, or causes you even deeper grief. There will be time to claim a more healing perspective. However a strong religious faith does not make us immune to intense pain and sorrow. Furthermore, emotional and spiritual anguish is not a sign of a weak faith. Although a personal religious perspective will be very comforting, it will not shield us from the task of grieving and the struggle with feelings of anger, depression and despair that are a normal part of grief.

The following excerpt from Elizabeth Yates' *Up the Golden Stair* appeared several years ago in our hospice news letter. She helps us accept the need to be with the pain at first and not push immediately for answers.

> "No matter how brave we think we are, or think we can be, we must call sorrow by its right name and see it for what it is. Only then can we avail ourselves of the treasure that is hidden in the folds of its dark cloak. I think that we should not, by any twist of the words we use, minimize what we are going through, what anyone goes through, when death enters upon life and removes a member of our circle, family—close or friendship-wide. There will be time enough to ponder the event, to philosophize about it, to discover its significance. Now, the bleak fact stands: a light has gone out; wherever it may be shining, it is here no longer."

MY MOST POWERFUL PRAYER

At the instant I knew our Eric had been killed, after the "flash ahead" of our future without him, I prayed, "O.K., God, you've got your work cut out for you. Get busy." This was not a fancy or particularly respectful prayer as prayers go. It was not my usual prayer of praise. It was a respectful recognition that I would need help. It was actually an imperative sentence as if I was telling a kid whose room was a disaster, "Well, you've got your work cut out for you. Get busy." Yet I knew in that moment of supreme testing that I could expect His help that way. It was the most powerful prayer experience of my life, for I knew I had gotten the message across and had the assurance that God would take it from there.

I was so fortunate because I had my theology of suffering in place before I needed it. Thus, I was spared the unbelievable anguish of "Why did God let this happen? What kind of God lets children die?"

I personally do not believe God intends premature death. I don't believe he directs or initiates suffering; we seem to do a pretty good job of doing that for ourselves. I believe in order to create a world where chaos doesn't rule, The laws of nature which keep our world stable are by nature consistent and can't be suspended every time someone is in death's way. God can't prevent death or the fateful chain of events that lead to catastrophe.

Yet, I believe our suffering matters terribly to God, and He is on our side in all of this, understanding our humanness, including the temptations and suffering we experience. I think He knows what it's like for us when we feel forsaken. I believe God would be the first one to weep with us and hold us, to mourn himself the loss of those whose lives here are earth could still serve His world so well. Sometimes, I look at things from God's point of view, and in all humility try to get into the mind of God. I think of His saying something like, "I'm sorry, that I couldn't avert that tragedy, that I couldn't spare you the suffering you have with this loss, but I will help you get through this. I'll send wonderful, compassionate people into your life, who, on my behalf, can comfort you. For I am a God of comfort and life. For I have created you all with the capacity to forge from sorrow a special community of caring and love."

A COSMIC PLAN FOR SURVIVAL

One thought has occurred to me so often during the many times I've had to grieve, that it's gained validity for me through the years. It seems to me that we wouldn't be created with the ability to love so much that we could hurt so deeply when that loved one died if there were not also created in our very being a way to survive, to keep on living. Otherwise, it seems to me that civilization would have mourned itself to death eons ago.

I tried to comfort my children with this intuitive belief during the days following their brother's death, but I knew it couldn't make sense to them. And, it didn't. But, three years later, Greta approached me one day and asked, "Mom, do you remember what you said when Eric died about their being something built into us, created in people to help them survive?" I nodded. And then I heard the wonderful words every parent cherishes. "You were right, Mom. I couldn't have believed it then, but it's much better now." I found that we parents who worry so about our children's ability to "get better" can also weep tears of thanksgiving.

During the first awful year, you must take steps to survive holidays and anniversaries and make deliberate attempts to cushion children in their grief. Every little effort you make marks a victory, for you've helped yourself cope. You're getting to the other shore. And, that's good news.

I
Scrapbook Scenes

1982—High School Graduation

1981—Working on his Car

1966—Early Car Drawing!

"Life: good as it is given"

1968—Family Christmas Photo

2001—My Husband and I

2002—Katrina, Karl and Greta
"More than Survivors"

CHAPTER 7

WHEN OTHERS LET YOU DOWN
WHEN OTHERS LIFT YOU UP

As if your valiant efforts to hold things together for yourself and others aren't enough to cope with, it ALWAYS happens—someone lets you down, fails at your time of greatest need. It can be a co-worker, acquaintance, the check out lady at the super market, the too busy receptionists at the doctor's. It may be a trusted friend or close family member; any might fall short of our expectations and requirements. Everyone in every group I've ever worked with has his own story, a story he can't forget, a story that can't be rewritten, a story that will always be part of the kaleidoscope of impressions and memories of this trying time.

Your friends will surprisingly say or do "the wrong thing," thereby giving you the impression that they don't know or don't care about your terrible pain. "I returned to work a week after my wife's death, and my boss never said a word. In fact, no one in the office even asked how I was doing. It was work as usual."

"She had the nerve to tell me it was all God's will and He never gives us more than we can bear."

"My mother says I should stop crying and feeling sorry for myself and get on with my life. Doesn't she realize it's only been a month since he died?"

"I didn't hear from my boyfriend for weeks after my Mom died, and then he simply calls and starts talking about this rafting trip he and his work buddies had been on, and 'how about we go out this week end; I've really missed you.' I told him about Mom's death thinking he'd been gone and didn't know. But, he had known. He casually replied, 'Yea, I read about the accident in the paper'. When I don't answer, he breezily adds,

'Oh, yea, I'm sorry she died. I'm just not good at that sort of thing'. After I hung up I cried a river of tears 'cause I realized he wasn't the one I wanted to pin my hopes on. It was over."

"I called my best friend when Mother was dying and asked her to come help, but she refused, saying she had her own bad times and was suffering more than I was." "I just can't believe it. The person I was absolutely sure I could count on wouldn't come." The catalogue of anger and pain can go on and on; you probably have your own entries.

The "why" they mess up is easily understood. Usually we're talking about well-intended people who are afraid of saying the wrong thing, who don't know what to do or say, who are afraid of sounding foolish. Many are uncomfortable or really scared of such intense emotional interactions. And, sadly, some may be just selfish, self-centered people who, like the boyfriend, are utterly "clueless."

The irony is that these are usually the "good guys," you know, the ones on our side who wear the white hats. Understandable as this rationale may be, however, when they don't support and help us, the pain can be devastating, the knowledge that they abandoned or ignored us can kill a relationship. So, it's essential that you find a way to handle this stress, or all your energy will we funneled into this cauldron of anger and hurt, energy you so desperately need for healing.

THE CRUELTY OF STRANGERS

I found that some of my greatest pain has been caused by innocent strangers; I learned that a simple, casual incident could render me breathless with anger. A few years after Eric's death, I had knee surgery, a simple out-patient procedure. The day before the scheduled operation, I reported on schedule for the usual tests and pre-op check up. A young, perky, nurse came in to check my vital signs and take a case history. With clipboard in hand and her pen ready, she briskly filled in the required questionnaire. It seemed she required my medical history from day one, all for a simple arthroscopic knee surgery. But, I was cooperative. She rattled off the questions and got to: "How many pregnancies?" "Four," I replied. Then, "How many children?" "Three," I answered calmly, but I hadn't been prepared for that one. "Oh," she waited patiently, pen poised expectantly above the clipboard, a math whiz demanding an explanation for such an obvious discrepancy.

"One died," I gritted my teeth and looked her in the eye. "Oh," she said, and obviously reassured that her math skills were not lacking, she moved on to the next question. When her forms were completed, she simply walked out, with some comment that they would want to have a second urinalysis.

I was shattered, scared at the intensity of my pain and anger. How dare this twit of a girl, this complete stranger, how dare she have the power to make me say out loud the most terrible pain of my life, my most private grief? And, then show no response at all and just sashay out of the room? Later, when I was calmer, I thought I should have answered her confusion over the child math with "Well, you know how it is with the runt of a litter." Thank goodness that crazy response came after she was gone.

But, usually the offense is committed by someone you have to interact with regularly. Consider whether or not this was a one time oversight by a friend or relative who is usually supportive. In the past has this person usually been thoughtful and sensitive? Could you usually count on him during bad times? If this is the case, let him know of your hurt, be kind, and move on.

SO, WHERE DO I GO FROM HERE?

First of all, remember that you're especially sensitive and vulnerable to everything right now, a bunch of exposed, raw nerves that hurt from the simplest touch. There are many situations where you can just overlook the hurt, and be a bit tolerant and philosophical about other folks' human frailties. Like you, they may be trying to do the best they can at this point. If you're fortunate enough to be in a support group, you can blow off steam there and be assured they will more than understand your rage and disappointment.

However, you don't need to remain silent and feel like a victim in all situations. You're entitled to let people know, kindly, how you feel, what you need, and how their behavior has affected you especially if this will threaten future relationships. You don't let them know by throwing a tantrum, screaming, name calling, or shooting them, tempting as these scenarios may seem at the moment.

You can try this time-tested pattern, focusing on the hurtful behavior, not on judging the person. "When you didn't phone or visit me after my husband died, I felt so hurt. It was as if our friendship didn't matter any more." This honest complaint certainly beats, "You selfish self centered wretch. No friend of mine would be so insensitive."

Still, it can be understandably tempting to see this insensitivity as the last straw and to completely sever relationships with this person now. But it's wiser if you don't make long-range judgments about any relationships or any irrevocable decision at this time. Put such momentous decisions on the back burner.

For now, no matter how much you hate it, accept that this is a new world of pain and loss that others can't possibly comprehend. So, in a way it's understandable that they can unknowingly really let you down. I'm afraid it's an added grief you have to absorb when you are so vulnerable and needy. And, life already seems so unfair. For now, use your grieving energy to mourn your loved one, the person most deserving of your suffering. And then, keep heading to shore.

YET, IF THEY ONLY KNEW . . . . IT TAKES SO LITTLE TO HELP SO MUCH

Thankfully, for every person who lets you down, there are many whose kindnesses and awkward attempts to bring comfort will lift you up and bring hope that it won't always be so wretched. It's like coming across unexpected buoys in the churning waters that you can grasp for brief moments of rest and be reminded that there will be a shore somewhere. However comforting someone, knowing what to say is always so difficult. We aren't sure if we'll say the "right" thing or just make it worse. The reasons we so often fail to say anything are understandable, even to us who felt injured by the silence of others.

"I'm afraid I'll say the wrong thing."

"Maybe I'll make it worse."

"It'll be so emotional; maybe she'll start crying and then what do I do?"

"What if he asks me why this happened? I don't have any answers."

HOWEVER, TO IGNORE THE LOSS AND SAY NOTHING IS NOT AN OPTION.

The irony is that so little is required to comfort at this time. What the bereaved require is simply that you acknowledge their loss. Simply say,

"I'M SORRY." I still feel so inadequate offering these plain words when I ache to be able to say something more profound, more meaningful, something that will really make a difference. But I have learned from long experience and from the authoritative voices of so many that there are no magic words; simple, heartfelt statements are fine. They do the job. So, here's the drill.

WHAT DO I SAY? HERE'S THE SECRET FORMULA
(Just fill in the blanks)

This is what you say. It is not hard. It is a good thing to do, and it will help. You can write the formula on a small flash card and keep it in your billfold.

"Hello (name of griever), I'm so sorry to hear about (name of deceased)'s death." Say this clearly and firmly, without rushing. Maintain eye contact and then allow a time of silence. There, now that's not too difficult to remember and if you know how to pronounce the participants' names and get them in the right order, it's not too taxing.

You 've earned your "A". Now, if you're going for extra credit, read on. Wait for the griever to nod or respond. Do not rush, or desperately try to fill the void with jabber and cliches. If you can manage a light touch or pat on the shoulder or arm, you get extra credit. A gentle touch alone, providing the human connectedness that comforts more than words, may be quite sufficient. If there's been a long illness, I sometimes add, "You've really had a long, hard time, haven't you?." And a simple "We're thinking about you," gets the important message across. You've given what they need most.

GRIEVING ON THE JOB

By the way, you're entitled to the same consideration as you struggle to cope with the demands "on the job". Surely it makes sense to recognize that these same words of acknowledgment and comfort are warranted in the workplace. But people assume that the struggles of one's personal life occur in a time and place completely separate. It's true that work must go on "as usual", services supplied, customers satisfied, and the usual deadlines met; however, after a loss, the inescapable demands of grief are part of the workplace whether we want it to be so or not. The supervisor should find a private time to speak personally with a returning employee, offering condolences, and asking directly what can be done to cushion the demands on the job, to make the work load less stressful for the next several weeks. There may be circumstances surrounding the loss, as in a suicide, that may be so painful that an employee might ask that no one offer condolences or mention his loss. Such a request must be honored if that will make this time any easier. It's better to talk one on one with the bereaved rather than in a group situation where the employee could feel vulnerable being "in the spotlight" at such a trying time. Still, every co-worker should at the very least in some way simply acknowledge the loss. They need only know THE FORMULA and just be sure they're up to speed on the name and relationship of the person who died.

My husband functioned pretty independently in his work (environmental research) at the time of Eric's death. But, he deliberately postponed projects that required concentration and precise deliberation for a couple of months. Fortunately, because of a previous reassignment, he was working in a separate location, where he could just lay his head down on his lab bench when he needed to "hurt" for a minute or two in privacy.

Two and a half months after Eric's death, I returned to teaching classes I had taught for nine years. I knew the material so well, had materials and lesson plans well in hand as I started the school year. But, it was as if I were teaching it all for the first time, impossibly difficult to decide how to schedule tests, how to evaluate assignments I had handled so professionally for years. It took a monumental effort to focus day by day. Actually, my greatest fear as I started the school year was that I'd have a student named "Eric" whom I'd have to call on by name. To my enormous relief, there were no "Erics" in my classes. I now know that some sort of legitimate leave during early weeks of mourning is as important as maternity leave.

THE WONDERFUL KINDNESS OF STRANGERS

You don't have to be a friend or close acquaintance to offer enormous comfort. When I look back on the months following our summer of heartbreak, I especially recall the gifts of compassion and kindness we received from virtual strangers, people I didn't know well at all. Three incidents were especially moving and healing. Although we are Protestants, many parents and friends from the Catholic school where I taught sent

Perpetual Mass cards that they had gone to the expense and effort of arranging for Eric. I was comforted knowing that someplace, these loving prayers, some from people I didn't know, were being offered on his behalf. It mattered that these people chose within the framework of their own faith to support and comfort us.

There's also a Jewish occasion of remembering the dead, a day of remembrance called Yahrzeit. Not being Jewish, I did not realize they could recognize someone outside of their own congregation. Louie's former secretary brought him a program of their synagogue service in which she had offered Eric's name. So there was the list of those to be remembered in the Kaddish prayer for the dead, "Abraham, Bessman, Cohen, Dietz, **Liljedahl**, Schuman, etc." I had known this lady only as a patient voice on the phone when I tried to contact my husband at work. Still, the precious gift she offered from her faith and her very soul mattered. To her it was a *mitsvah*, but to us a blessing.

THE GIFT OF A STRANGER'S TEARS

Before Eric died, our daughter had volunteered to be part of a control group for a National Institute of Health research study on manic-depressive behavior in young women. She responsibly felt she couldn't just drop out without compromising the research project. The study required that parents of those selected for the control group be interviewed to ascertain, I presume, that they didn't have symptoms of this mental illness themselves. Our interview was three months after Eric died. (Remember, the time you hit that "wall" of forever) The study coordinators had been informed about Eric's accident and our reluctance to be interviewed then, but it was necessary to proceed.

My husband and I were interviewed separately by the assistant to the physician in charge of the study. She sat across the room from me with her clipboard asking the necessary questions to determine my emotional status. When she got to questions about depression, I said something like, "I don't think I'm usually a depressed person, at all. But, things have been so hard these past weeks I don't know how to answer you. I'm very sad, and depressed now, but I know it's not how it used to be." Then I glanced across the room to ascertain her reaction. (My past experience with interrogating women armed with clipboards made me understandably wary). But, to my amazement, She was sitting quietly as tears silently rolled down her face. Seeing my surprise, she quietly wiped her eyes and said, "I'm just so sorry you had to go through all that." That was all; we proceeded with the interview. But, it was more than enough. Shedding tears for a stranger's pain is more than enough, believe me.

LET YOUR INSTINCTS BE YOUR GUIDE

The reason many friends, acquaintances, and these strangers provided such monumental comfort was that they trusted their instincts, just did what seemed to come naturally.

The day after Eric's death, a neighbor called. I knew Roz because our kids were the same ages and we had done car pool stuff, but I actually knew her children more. At that time, she was public relations director for the University of Maryland, a very demanding, high pressure job. So, suddenly she called and said, "Joan, I've already arranged to take off from work today. If you'd like, I'd be so glad to help you with Eric's obituary. And I'll be able to get the obituary and death notice into the Washington Post." Obituary? That hadn't even entered our mind. There was just no way on earth that we could have suddenly written an obituary for a nineteen year old boy who was alive and healthy just twenty four hours before. The very thought was prelude to hysteria. Well, Roz did it for us. In fact, she drove us to the funeral home and talked to them about death notices: I have no idea what the actual words were about because surely none it applied to our fractured lives. She worked most of the day, polishing the newspaper article, helping us find a picture to include, checking back a few times to see if we had something else to add. She used her talents, did her best, and gave us the most precious of gifts.

A few weeks after later, I learned that neighbors on our block whom we did not know too well at that time, who certainly had never known Eric, had sat in their front yard the afternoon of his service maintaining their vigil on the houses in our neighborhood, just in case an enterprising thief decided to take advantage of a time when so many wouldn't be home. It was like having someone house sit during a wedding. A very wise, very quiet, and very thoughtful gesture.

Still the friends who helped most weren't those who gave advice or told us things we should or shouldn't do. They were the ones who simply came and listened and listened and listened, their heartfelt quietness and hugs more healing and helpful than any words.

I'm not intending to cover all of the many ways we can help others at time of loss, but just to highlight some things people did that truly brought comfort and hope, and with that a desperately needed assurance that we were not alone. Despite the times you are disappointed or greatly let down, be on the watch for and savor such precious lifelines that will also guide you to the distant shore.

CHAPTER 8

GOOD NEWS—THERE'S HELP AROUND AND WITHIN

"Getting better" doesn't just happen. It always takes so long, a year, or maybe years, of tears, but you don't have to reside on an "Isle of Endless Grief" forever. Don't overlook the resources around you that can ease this passage. Most friends and relatives do come through and are eager to help if they just know what to do, like taking the children to a movie or helping you shampoo rugs. So ask directly and specifically for what you need. "It would really help if you could take my mother to her doctor's appointment next Wednesday, or pick Jenny up after her piano lesson tomorrow afternoon." Friends will be relieved knowing ways they can "do something" to help. Don't be heroic and do it alone; instead, be responsible and use the best resources available, like support groups.

THE MAGIC OF SUPPORT GROUPS

The solace offered by a support group can be a saving grace. I did not know about such groups when my parents died or when our son died, but, to be honest, maybe I wouldn't have attended. Letting a group of strangers witness my deepest pain, and listening to their stories of misery wouldn't have appealed to me. Since then I've worked for more than a dozen years with support groups, and admit I was wrong, big time wrong.

What can happen in a strong support group is nothing short of magic. A group of about twelve or so strangers from very diverse backgrounds, with no common history, meet for about six weeks and share their greatest pain. It takes courage to risk being so vulnerable, but they find the comfort of knowing they all speak the same language, that of loss and suffering. The compassion

I've noticed in such groups is almost holy. Many forge the strongest bonds in shared suffering, form lasting friendships. Do yourself a favor if you're having a hard time. Get a bereavement connection. Most hospitals can recommend resources if they don't have a program in place. I've included a list of some specialized support groups in the Appendix, (p. 91).

AND NOW FOR THE "REST OF THE STORY"

In Chapter 3 (page 43) I told of the heartbreaking bereavement group in Washington, D.C. I helped to cope with the violent deaths of sons, husbands, even a teenage grandson. Our six sessions followed the usual group routine, mainly focusing on sharing, talking, listening to the saddest of homicide stories, too outrageous to bear.

About eighteen months later, I received a surprise phone call from Sharon, one of the group participants asking if I could come meet with the group one more time. I agreed, pleased to be asked and curious to see how they had managed for the past year and a half.

I heard the welcome sounds of happy chatter as I entered our old meeting room and entered. With smiles, hugs, and outcries of joy they surrounded me. Dumbfounded and speechless at this unexpectedly festive reception, I was escorted to my old position at the conference table while the rest took their accustomed seats. And then they explained "the rest of the story."

"Our sessions with you were so good, we all decided to just keep on meeting and talking among ourselves. So we've been meeting here every Saturday for the past year and a half." Voices bubbled with energy as the narrative moved from one excited woman to another. "We've become real 'sisters', sharing not only our grief and the hard memories but all the other stuff in our lives. Sure we remember the awful anniversaries, the holidays, and the crying times, but we also do fun things and have happy times together. Best of all, we count on each other and call each other any time of the day or night.

"We just wanted to thank you again for helping and let you know how great we're doing. Bet you never expected to see this sorry bunch of heart-sick, angry gals so happy and helping each other in life".

Six sessions of enormously grief-stricken women ready to be to talk openly about their pain had metamorphosed into a healthy, compassionate sisterhood.

They had experienced the power of a support group. It can also work for you. And that's the rest of the story.

WAYS YOU CAN HELP YOURSELF

But your greatest advocate and powerful resource is your own strength; you can help yourself find the best path for your own recovery. Here are some suggestions that people from our groups repeatedly emphasized.

ADVICE—TAKE IT OR LEAVE IT

It's the American way, to offer advice whether it's asked for or not. Just mention that you're cutting back on calories and everyone has a food plan for you. Let a man just suggests that the transmission in his car is a bit noisy, and every other guy has an opinion about how to proceed. So, in this helpful All American tradition, you can expect all kinds of advice. And, yes, I know this book, like many others, is full of it. Actually, much advice is not only well intended, but very astute and helpful. For example, everyone would advise you not to make any unnecessary major decisions during the first year after a loss. Abrupt changes just add more stress, and you really aren't thinking as clearly as you believe you are.

Advice is something to listen to, and consider carefully; however, you must make the final decision of what feels best, what seems to be the best course for you. Simply say, "I appreciate your interest and your suggestions have merit, but that doesn't work for me now." Maybe you will have to be super diplomatic and say, "I'll have to think about that for a while before I'd go ahead with that idea," to give you an out for ignoring advice. But you bear the final responsibility for how you manage this time of sorrow, so the final choice must be yours. Don't be afraid to try it your way, to trust your instincts. That's my advice.

GETTING RID OF POSSESSIONS

And always there's the wretched task of sorting though possessions. When Eric died, we determined that we would get the heartbreaking chore out of the way, but it didn't work then. We did some sorting, but it was more than we could bear. It would have been irresponsible to make those decisions considering our precarious emotional status. You too may have conflicting ideas about what to do with your loved one's clothes and possessions, but you'll figure out what's best for you. There's no time limit, no deadline. Many find that after a few weeks they experience a burst of energy that enables them to get the job done, but you may not get around to it for a year or more. Just don't worry about it or let it hang over you. You'll sense when it's best for you.

FINDING A HOME FOR A BOY'S CAR

There was one possession of Eric's that was unbearable for us to part with, his British racing green Spitfire sports car. It had been a wreck when he bought it, but he had been able to restore it into a nice specimen. It had taken a lot of work sanding and painting it, finding a new windshield and scrounging for reasonably priced parts. The license plate read "Sam I" which stood for (good) Samaritan I, for his great joy and pride was cruising the Beltway and helping out those who were stalled. Of course, it wasn't safe, but he was cautious. He had jumper cables, tire inflator cans, first aid stuff, a can of gasoline, and water supplies carefully packed into the small trunk. Since he had a real mechanical feel and instinct for cars and had taken an auto mechanics class, this Good Samaritan endeavor made sense. Of course, he was saving for his dream, a four wheel drive car or truck that he could legitimately take out during blizzards when appeals were made for such vehicles.

But, this little car brought him such joy, such satisfaction. After he died, we just couldn't, we just absolutely couldn't, let it go. Actually it was in our driveway for almost three years. Occasionally prospective buyers would stop by the house and ask if it were for sale, but my husband didn't want to do that; he'd tell them he thought he'd do more work on it and maybe drive it himself. But, that didn't happen. During the first winter, he ordered a nylon cover, sort of a big shower cap for cars, and for two years, Sam I lay protected in this gray cloth shroud. We didn't feel compelled to act, and that was wise. Although it broke our hearts to have its too quiet presence in our driveway, we did what was best for us.

Finally, Greta found out about a teen age boy who attended Eric's church and desperately needed a car for school, a boy who loved working on cars, but had no money. "Someone like Eric, a really great kid," she assured us. Of course, this was the solution. How wonderful that we could just give him the car, a possession of Eric's we could never have sold. The overjoyed boy and his father brought a car trailer and Louie helped them gently herd the Spitfire up the ramp, to go with its new master. Our heartache was tempered knowing this was exactly what Eric would have wanted. I was glad we waited until it was right.

JOURNALING—WRITE IT HOW IT IS

Many people recommend the support you can find through journaling, that is, by keeping a notebook where you write down what you're thinking or what you've been thinking, maybe every day or maybe just whenever you're feeling low. It is in the process of writing that we often discover meaning, and clarify our thoughts. Maybe you've noticed this when you start writing to a good friend and end up writing about all kinds of stuff that's going on. So, journaling, jotting down your impressions, your feelings, your worries can help you find a place to put the anger and the sadness. Here's where you can write the scalding letters you don't mail. Here's a good place to write a letter to your loved one, to express the thoughts you didn't have a chance to say. The questions and answers that can aid your recovery often come from times like these. Remember, you're not writing for your high school English teacher, the one with the red pencil. If writing is hard for you to do because you're not used to it, then try talking to a tape recorder instead. Keep the tapes separate and date them. Your journal or tapes can be a private healing conversation with yourself.

Remember, you are the prime authority on you. You owe no-one any apology for grieving your own way, on your own schedule. Unclaimed power for recovery is there, and you deserve it.

CHAPTER 9

CHAOS TO RENEWAL: WHEN IT GETS BETTER

Since the circumstances surrounding the death of our loved one are so traumatic and overpowering, as is our story of Eric's death, we tend to expect that the recovery phase will also be a dramatic revelation, a climax to our story clearly symbolizing we've won the grief marathon and are well on the way to healing. After months or of turmoil and the trials of coping, it seems we should have earned the satisfaction, of a background fanfare of trumpets and the moving poignant strains of violins.

But "NO," it doesn't usually work that way. Rather, it gets better in "bits and pieces." But, believe me, those "bits and pieces" are miracles in themselves. It's as if you've been in the bottom of a deep pit of despair, the opening at the top obscured by darkened cloud cover. Then, finally, the clouds above this pit move away, and there's just enough light for you to get a clearer view of your situation. Gradually you notice some unevenly spaced footholds or indentions in the hard packed earthen wall leading toward the top of the prison, and you slowly, with great care, make the long climb to the top. Sometimes your foot slips and you frantically grapple for a niche below to halt your fall, but you eventually regain your balance and composure and tackle the next fragile step. To me, each faltering, yet determined step upward is worthy of great fanfare, a powerful affirmation that you are going to reach the top.

And so, very gently and almost imperceptibly, you will find to your amazement that you're getting better. Perhaps the pain isn't there every single minute, or maybe it's not as intense and powerful as before.

About four months after Eric's accident, I was walking to my car after a day of teaching. Suddenly, I realized I had gone the entire day without grieving. I had gotten up in the morning, gone to the bathroom, had breakfast, and driven to school like "ordinary people." I had taught my ninth grade English classes and enjoyed talking to my colleagues as it had been "way back in the old days." I'd been briefly released from the heaviness, the fringes of sorrow that had been forever a part of my world. It felt like "Hallelujah", a glimpse of the solid shore ahead, of life, of hope. For those few hours, I had not been in bondage to grief; I didn't know at the time that I was experiencing a brief foretaste of the final phase.

If you're in the early months of your loss, I'd just ask you to trust that this *will* happen. But if you can just trust that it will eventually happen, perhaps this will offer hope, a broken down life raft that still floats as you head for shore.

Books on grief usually offers the phrase "acceptance", "reinvestment in life", or "integration of the loss" to define the time when things get better. Many like the term "acceptance", for it suggests they have accepted the reality of the loss, worked through the harsher feelings, and are ready to get on with life. This term doesn't work for me, personally, for there's a place deep inside where I can and will never accept my son's not being with us in the here and now of our lives. The phrase "integrating the loss" fits my experience better. Finally the loss isn't overpowering me, claiming my energy and attention, requiring me to be wary and defensive. It's now woven into the fabric of my life, and my life is in charge. It's as if somber shades are still in the background, but the brighter colors are now in the foreground and the fabric is beautiful again. I'm including a copy of a diagram of the grief process I've used in our groups at Holy Cross Hospital. It illustrates how things changed for me, not in a straight line, but two steps forward and one back, good days or weeks of confidence and then a wretched week of sliding back, and then getting better and better.

The Grief Wheel

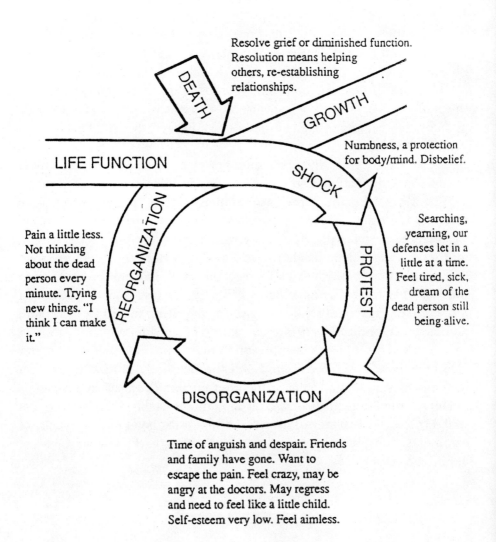

Resolve grief or diminished function. Resolution means helping others, re-establishing relationships.

DEATH

GROWTH

LIFE FUNCTION

Numbness, a protection for body/mind. Disbelief.

SHOCK

Searching, yearning, our defenses let in a little at a time. Feel tired, sick, dream of the dead person still being alive.

PROTEST

REORGANIZATION

Pain a little less. Not thinking about the dead person every minute. Trying new things. "I think I can make it."

DISORGANIZATION

Time of anguish and despair. Friends and family have gone. Want to escape the pain. Feel crazy, may be angry at the doctors. May regress and need to feel like a little child. Self-esteem very low. Feel aimless.

Based on a diagram from the Grief Education Institute, Englewood, CO

THE LITTLE SIGNS THAT PROMISE HOPE

Sometimes events that affirm our progress can be unexpected surprises. A friend told me that a few months after her husband's death, she had to pay their auto insurance premium. She studied the material and realized it wasn't such a good deal. So, she researched and found another insurance company that was preferable and changed. "I can't believe I did it all myself. I would never have thought to question my husband's choice. I did it." She sounded like a kid taking off on her first two-wheeler. Another widow dropped a piece of her bridgework down the drain. She rummaged around and finding her husband's box of tools, found some "things" that she used to dismantle the pipes. And, to her credit and pride, she retrieved the lost item. Both women found power they hadn't even known they had. They had learned to "make it on their own."

A widow in our group had just noted what would have been their 54th wedding anniversary in a wonderful, nurturing joyous marriage despite the fact that he had been ill for a long time and she had lovingly cared for him before he died. She told us at one meeting with a sparkle in her eyes, "The other day I was at the mall with some friends and suddenly realized I didn't *have* to get back at a certain time to check on Ed. I felt so free, I just went shopping with my friends and bought myself something expensive that I didn't need, and we had dinner. I'm almost ashamed to say it (that Big G thing again), but I had a wonderful time." She added wistfully. "But, I hate going back to the empty house. How I wish he were there."

About eighteen months after Eric's death, I was attending a college pot-luck Christmas get together. I had contributed my special Sloppy Joe recipe. When someone commented on how good it was, I replied, "This was my son's most favorite recipe." A few minutes later I was hit by the realization that:

1. I had obviously located the recipe card titled "Eric's Sloppy Joes" without any difficulty; in the beginning, I couldn't have even looked at the words.
2. I had gone to the store and bought the stuff without freaking out like before.
3. I had enjoyed making his favorite recipe just as I had back in the old days.

Best of all, I didn't feel sad realizing this; I just felt grateful: I even heard some trumpet fanfare in the distance. I'm including this recipe here. It's easy, maybe even bereavement-proof.

ERIC'S FAVORITE SLOPPY JOES

1 pound ground chuck	1 cup chopped onion
1 cup catsup	2 teaspoons prepared mustard
1 tablespoon vinegar	1 teaspoon each, sugar and salt

Brown the ground chuck and chopped onions in skillet.
Mix in the other ingredients and simmer for twenty minutes.

The recipe success was a week before Christmas, and then Christmas wasn't so great. I ached to tell Eric how much everyone loved his favorite recipe, and hear his enthusiastic, "Why sure, Mom, what did you expect?" I swooped from a roller coaster high of success to the valley of aching and missing. I was reminded that hard days had followed the good day I had at school. Yet, good days did gradually return. After a long time, the "normal" days were more and more frequent until they far outnumbered any sad ones. We don't get better in a straight line just as recovery from a physical illness or surgery goes in spurts.

There are still moments when I can momentarily spiral down into the deep well of grief where the old pain clutches and tears, but I now know I will soon rise out of that darkened depth which doesn't have a permanent claim or the final word. My "getting better" is now in charge.

HOW DO I KNOW I AM GETTING BETTER?

Everyone harbors the uneasy fear that maybe, just maybe he won't get better. Everyone wonders at some time if he is "doing O.K." and really managing the unwelcome challenge. A couple of weeks before our first Christmas after Eric's death, I called my widowed aunt in Texas. She picked up on the sadness underneath my words and offered gently, "I was talking the other day to so and so, my friend whose husband died a few years ago. And she just reminded me that we cope better and better as time goes on." At first it didn't sound so profound. But, later, her words seemed just perfect, just what I needed to hear.

"Well," I thought, "I can "cope." That's not too much. I don't have to make things perfect yet, I don't have to make the ache go away, I don't have to make Christmas like it was, I just need to cope, and I can do that." Knowing and accepting that you need only cope and trusting that you can do this is a fine sign that you're on the right track.

THE HEALING PRESENCE OF HUMOR

I once asked Karl, our older son, how he was managing during a stressful time. His reply was, "I'm O.K. Mom. I'm keeping one nostril above water." That's another way of putting it, of saying you're barely managing to head for shore, but you're still afloat. As I worked to revise this book, my younger daughter remarked with her wry sense of humor, "Mom, to make any book sell nowadays you have to have something in it about diet, like "the low-carb grief diet." Her older sister laughed and said I should also include some workout plans as well, if I hoped for any marketing success, and we all broke out laughing. Believe me, there wasn't any humor or joking, when I wept through my first draft. Things have changed for good when we can laugh again.

THE PROFESSIONAL VIEW—NOT SO DIFFERENT

Professional mental health counselors use standards nearly as simple as my son's. When Sigmund Freud, the father of psychotherapy, was asked what were the criteria for mental stability he remarked that a person was managing fine if he could "lieben und arbeiten", love and work. Counselors still use these standards of emotional health today. Now, by "love" we don't mean romantic entanglements. It means that you're able to keep relationships going without alienating everyone. You maintain contact with people and can interact in a reasonable manner. You can stand to be with others. "Work" doesn't just refer to the job; it includes all the tasks one must perform at home as well as at work. Do you eventually get the beds made and laundry done? Do you eventually get the haircut and make the dentist appointment? Do you manage to *keep* your job? Have you managed to stay married? You shouldn't expect to perform these tasks at your previous level of competence or incompetence, as the case may be, nor should others expect you to. You just need to muddle through with one nostril above water, confident that you're getting nearer and nearer to the not so distant shore.

ON BECOMING A HERO

Trusting this process is always a monumental act of faith. It is raw faith that dares believe that, despite the despair and terror, things will get better. I'm proud of many accomplishments in my life: surviving my first year teaching, returning to graduate school at a more mature age, driving when necessary to visit someone in a Washington, D. C. hospital though I hate the drive. But I am most proud that I have grieved an unbearable loss thoroughly and honorably without bitterness. I have not only survived. I have prevailed.

And our family has prevailed though I'd never have believed such a possibility on the day our worlds changed forever. Katrina is a pediatric nurse especially informed and responsive to families who have lost a child. Despite resurfacing grief, she did a monumental critical, expert job in the final editing of this book. Greta and her husband have done missionary work in Africa and China; the dream she and her brother once shared does live on. Our son Karl is a biology professor at a community college. After our fiftieth wedding anniversary he arranged a family reunion at Rehoboth Beach, where years ago our family would vacation for two weeks every summer. And now, our eight grandchildren know the beach stories when their parents and Uncle Eric were young beachcombers and riders of the surf.

Ours is an accomplishment of heroic proportions. You too merit membership in our company of heroes. I can think of no better way to honor those we love; I can imagine no tribute more fitting.

THE GOLD STAYS

I believe we are like the beachcombers I've watched in the cool predawn hours, following the tides of the night, with their magnetometers searching for treasures large or small that have been left behind, buried just beneath the surface of the sand. There will be many ordinary shells to be discarded, and other flotsam which has been thrown back by a storm or the tide to also be passed over, as they patiently and diligently continue the quest for gold and other precious items.

And when they find precious items, possibly gold, some other valuable metal, perhaps a rare stone or trinket, they seem to instantly appreciate the worth of their treasures as they quickly brush clinging sands away and wash them off. Then they examine them in the sun's rays, and put them in a pouch for safe keeping.

In like manner you need not fear the journey ahead that as you reach that distant shore of recovery you'll forget the dear one who added such luster to your life, that the memories will fade with the pain. The pain will fade, softening into sadness, but I promise you, the treasure, the gold stays.

APPENDIX I

FINDING A SUPPORT GROUP

The most direct way to find a grief support group is to call your local hospital and ask for the phone number of the nearest hospice, or phone the National Hospice and Palliative Care Organization at 1-800-658-8898 for the locations of the nearest hospice. Then call the hospice and ask for information about local grief support groups. Also, many mortuaries supply information about local grief support groups.

In addition, you may wish to check with the following national organizations for the location of their local chapters and support groups, which are concerned with grief under special circumstances:

For child loss, contact—
The Compassionate Friends, Inc.
P. O. Box 3696
Oak Brook, IL 60522-3696
Toll-free: 877-969-0010 ph: 630-990-0010
http://www.compassionatefriends.org
Good for emotional support

For loss of a spouse, contact—
AARP's Widowed Person's Service
601 E St. NW
Washington, DC 20049
(202) 434-2260
More emphasis on meeting practical and social needs

For survivors of suicide, contact—
American Foundation for Suicide Prevention
New York, New York 10005
TOLL-FREE: 888-333-AFSP   phone: (212) 363-3500
http://www.afsp.org/survivor/groups.htm
   Offer a wide variety of help for survivors of suicide, including support groups

There are a great many Web sites intended to help those who grieve. To be more sure you access the best, search for them at the following indexes—

http://www.bereavementmag.com/resources/default
http://www.growthhouse.org/nhpco/
http://www.soberrecovery.com/links/griefandloss.html

APPENDIX II

AND NOW FOR YOUR STORY

I'm including a few questions for each chapter to encourage you to consider if and how my observations fit your experience. These "questions" are to help you reflect on, and perhaps clarify, your own experience. Maybe they will provide some ideas for your own journaling. If you are using this book in a bereavement group, it might help your leader initiate helpful discussions.

CHAPTER ONE: BUT I WASN'T READY
1. What is your earliest recollection of someone's death? How did adults act and explain it to you? What did these early experiences teach you about death and grieving?
2. How can a crisis like a death in the family help or harm family relationships?
3. How would you incorporate the realities of grieving and preparation for loss in the school curricula?
4. In what ways were you were unprepared or ill—informed when faced with a significant loss?

CHAPTER TWO: IN THE BEGINNING—CHAOS
1. What was it like when you heard about a loved one's death? What scenes or feelings flashed through your mind at that crucial time?
2. Were there ways in which you coped magnificently during the early weeks of your loss? Did others comment on your courage then or how beautifully you "handled" it? If so, how did you respond? What did you REALLY feel like saying?

3. Did you have the experience of "Hitting the wall" after a few weeks? If so, what was it like?
4. Did you have any "crazy" episodes like the grocery store?
5. Were tears a problem for you? Were your tears or lack of tears a problem for others? How did you let people know it was okay if you had to cry?
5. What does the phrase "surviving day by day" mean to you? Why is it such a great accomplishment?

CHAPTER THREE: YOU DON'T NEED BLOOD EVERYWHERE TO FEEL PAIN

1. How did adults react to your emotional outbursts when you were a child?
2. Are feelings of anger or guilt part of your grieving? Describe them.
3. Does my distinction between "guilt" and "remorse" make sense to you?
4. What emotions surrounding grief weren't mentioned or adequately explained in this chapter?
5. In what ways are we unfair in our expectations of men during a time of crisis? From your observations, how DO men grieve differently from women?
6. A crucial decision in the grief process is whether to go with the suffering and pain or to ignore it. What's your reaction to this observation?
7. Why might this chapter be considered one of the most crucial chapter in this book?

CHAPTER FOUR: THE STRESSES IN SPECIFIC LOSSES

1. What thoughts or observations DO you have in coping with a specific loss as parent, child, spouse that should be included in this chapter?
2. Have you known of any situations where there was a suicide? If so, how did people help and support the family? How did people fail?
3. Can you think of reasons why marriages are at such risk during the time of a death, especially following the death of a child ? What can a couple DO to strengthen a marriage at such a critical time?
4. Can you suggest other ways we can help children during the time of a major loss in the family?
5. Why are miscarriages and infant loss so overlooked? How can we comfort those who suffer such pain?
6. Is violent death a realistic topic for this book? Was some relevant material omitted here?

CHAPTER FIVE.　　　　　GRIEVING THE DEATH OF
AN UNLOVED ONE GRIEVING
THE DEATH OF THE RECKLESS

1. Should this chapter even be included in a book like this?
2. If you've had to wrestle with the task of grieving the death of an unkind or a reckless person, how did you handle it?
3. Write a letter to that person in your journal. Just what would you like to tell that person now?
4. Are any of the "unspeakable thoughts" I listed true in your experience? What are some others I should have included?
5. Some experts say that acknowledging the ambivalence in a relationship (the bad as well as good parts) is a major task of grieving. Can you write or talk about any faults your loved one had?
6. DO the three considerations or second thoughts in reflecting on the death of a reckless person at the end of this chapter make sense or are they just unrealistic expectations?

CHAPTER SIX:　　　　　COPING WITH CHILDREN, HOLIDAYS,
AND THE "WHY" OF IT ALL

1. What specific plans can you devise to help you cope with holidays during the first year? How can you offer help to others at this sad milestone?
2. What's the hardest part in managing birthdays and anniversaries for you? What specific things can you do or plan for that might make these easier?
3. How does your religious faith or tradition sustain you now? Is it harder to hold fast to your faith at this time? Easier?
4. What circumstances can make it really difficult to help children in the family adjust to death?
5. This chapter included just three areas of stress during a time of loss. What other situations can cause difficulty?

CHAPTER SEVEN:　WHEN OTHERS THEY LET YOU DOWN
WHEN OTHERS LIFT YOU UP

1. What are some ways people failed you at the time of your loss?
2. Write a letter to the person or people who upset you telling them just how you feel. You *do not need to mail it.*
3. I suggest that you put off any final decisions about breaking off a relationship at this time? How do you feel about this?

4. What fears or concerns make you uneasy about being with or helping someone who has just suffered a major loss?
5. In what ways did people help you or someone you knew at the time of a heartbreaking loss? Were there some special things someone did or said that really helped?
6. Has it been difficult getting back to work? How did co-workers or your boss make it easier? Were there any ways they made it more difficult?

CHAPTER EIGHT: GOOD NEWS—THE HELP
AROUND AND WITHIN

1. Do you have friends with whom you can openly share your feelings and sadness? If not, how can you find this necessary support?
2. Are there ways in which you have affirmed the best way for you to cope with your grief despite the advice and feelings of others who disagree?
3. What things do you do for yourself now that help you cope and just keep going?
4. Have you tried journaling?

CHAPTER NINE: WHEN IT GETS BETTER

1. What would "getting better" mean for you?
2. Does "Getting better by bits and pieces" make sense to you?
3. Think of a few little things, or "signs" that show you that you are actually getting just a little better.
4. In the first chapter I told you that, "You are stronger and wiser than you think." Do you believe this now?